KILIMANJARO &
MOUNT KENYA

KILIMANJARO & MOUNT KENYA

A CLIMBING AND TREKKING GUIDE

Cameron M. Burns

THE
MOUNTAINEERS

Published by
The Mountaineers
1001 SW Klickitat Way, Suite 201
Seattle, WA 98134

First edition: first printing 1998, second printing 1999

Published simultaneously in Great Britain by Cordee, 3a DeMontfort Street, Leicester, England, LE1 7HD

Manufactured in the United States of America

Edited by Mary Anne Stewart
Maps by Kerry L. Burns
Topos by Gray Mouse Graphics
Cover design by Kristy L. Welch
Book design, layout, typography by Jennifer Shontz

Cover photograph: *Kibo from Barranco hut area* (Photo © Cameron M. Burns) *Along the Machame Trail* (Photo © Cameron M. Burns) Frontispiece: *Mawenzi from Kibo Hut area, Marangu Route, Kilimanjaro* (Photo © Cameron M. Burns)

Library of Congress Cataloging-in-Publication Data
Burns, Cameron.
    Kilimanjaro & Mount Kenya: a climbing and trekking guide / Cameron Burns.
        p.   cm.
    Includes bibliographical references (p.   ) and index.
    ISBN 0-89886-557-3
    1. Mountaineering—Tanzania—Kilimanjaro, Mount—Guidebooks. 2. Mountaineering—Kenya—Kenya, Mount—Guidebooks. 3. Hiking—Tanzania—Kilimanjaro, Mount—Guidebooks. 4. Hiking—Kenya—Kenya, Mount—Guidebooks. 5. Kilimanjaro, Mount (Tanzania)—Guidebooks. 6. Kenya, Mount (Kenya)—Guidebooks. I. Title. II. Title: Kilimanjaro and Mount Kenya. III. Title: Kilimanjaro & Mt. Kenya. IV. Title: Kilimanjaro and Mt. Kenya.
    GV199.44.T342K553 1998
    796.52'2'0967826—dc21   97-45542
                                                                                CIP

*This book is dedicated to my two
wonderful sisters, Penelope and
Gillian, who never let me forget
I was their* little *brother.*

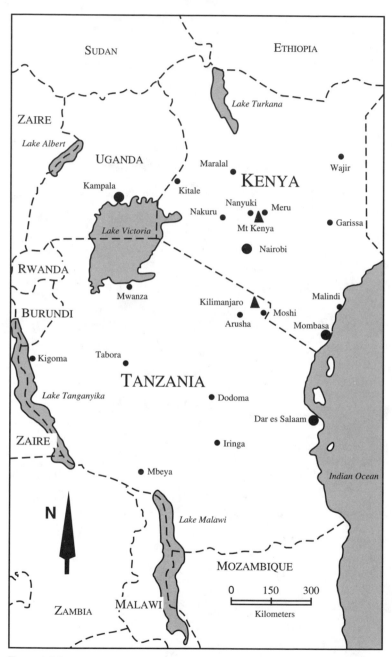

East Africa

CONTENTS

ACKNOWLEDGMENTS

This book would not have been possible without help from many people.

Bongo Woodley, Mount Kenya National Park warden, and Matthew Mombo, Kilimanjaro National Park warden, spent considerable time with me, answering even the simplest questions with patience and care.

Michael Wanjau and Zakayo Leparie followed up with me when Bongo was called out to fight fires on Mount Kenya. Their help was invaluable.

In Tanzania, the following people made my times in Moshi and on Kilimanjaro an absolute joy: Zainab and Roger Ansell, Omari Chambo, Mohammed Hemed, Allen Melickzedek Mremi, Sifuni Pallangyo, John Rafaeli, Hamadi Saidi, William and Michael Sandy, Sada Sherali, and Mohommed Ali Tenga.

In Kenya, the following people made my trips to Mount Kenya an exceptional experience: Lawrence Gitonga, Leonard Josphat, Ambrose Kirimi, Anthony Miriti Manene, Loyford Mutembei Mburia, Daniel Mugendi Rufas, and Marc and Benson at the Transit in Chogoria.

My main climbing partners put up with a lot of photo stops and seemingly silly sidetrips. For their patience, I thank my wife, Ann Robertson, and Benny Bach and Tristan Cooper.

Longtime Sierra climber Bart O'Brien's help with route descriptions and photographs on various Mount Kenya routes was invaluable.

Thanks also to Yvon Chouinard, Lindsay Griffin, Ian Howell, Doug Scott, and John Temple for their encouragement and photographs.

Other folks whose help has been invaluable include Iain Allan, Mike Baker, David Bristow, Jon Butler, Jean and Sabrina DeLataillade, Cory Ferguson and the team at BJ Adams & Co., Jim Freeman, Paul Gagner, Dion Goldsworthy, Wayne Gregory, Jesse Harvey, Leslie Henderson, Roger Jones, Theresa and Dennis Junt, Luke Laeser, Mel Macdonell, Alloyce Okello, Chris Pomeroy, Steve and Sandy Porcella, Dave Sessions, Bob and Elizabeth Ward, and, of course, my publishing world mentor, George Meyers.

My wonderful parents and parents-in-law, Kerry and Mary Burns and Bob and Sylvia Robertson, regularly helped my wife and me wrangle luggage through Denver's International Airport. Thanks!

All the folks at The Mountaineers Books were remarkably patient with me, especially Margaret Foster, Cindy Bohn, Jennifer Shontz, Taryn Himmelright, Mary Metz, Hally Swift, Thom Votteler, and, of course, Art Freeman.

Finally, a huge thank-you to editor Mary Anne Stewart, without whom this book would not be in English!

INTRODUCTION

It is often said that Africa is a land of contrasts.

It's a land where the driest deserts butt up against the wettest jungles; a place where the strongest creatures in the world can be seen tearing the flesh off the most beautiful; and a continent where the imported European view of things rubs hard up against the indigenous understanding of the world.

Similarly, Kilimanjaro, the highest peak on the African continent, is a mountain of contrasts.

Few peaks on the planet have the distinction of being a continental high point and an exotic destination: Kilimanjaro is both. At 5,895 meters (19,341 feet), Kilimanjaro is a must-climb on the hard-core mountaineer's list of objectives, as well as a colorful backdrop for dozens of famous literary works and films.

Perhaps more than anything, Kilimanjaro—and its sister peak, Mount Kenya—are contrasts in complexity.

From a distance, Kilimanjaro looks like nothing more than a big rounded hill, a large volcanic cone sawed off at the stump and left with few features of interest to technical climbers. Likewise, from most vantage points, Mount Kenya looks like not much more than a lopsided spire sitting above the Kenyan jungle.

Close examination reveals that both are not single-summited mountains, but multispired massifs. Indeed, rising thousands of meters above the surrounding jungles and plains, both mountains are their own ecosystems and create their own weather.

Specifically, Kilimanjaro is dominated by two major summits, Kibo (5,895 meters/19,341 feet) and Mawenzi (5,149 meters/16,893 feet), which are separated by an 11-kilometer-wide saddle. The rounded snow-covered summit of Kibo contrasts easily with the craggy rock spire of Mawenzi. And while many sides of the mountain offer gentle slopes to wander up, massive cliff bands like the fabulous Breach Wall present technical climbers with alpine testpieces. Some climbing routes on Kilimanjaro are mere strolls at high altitude. Others are long, serious, and very difficult undertakings, as challenging as anything in the world and requiring all a mountaineer's skill.

Likewise, the lopsided spire of Mount Kenya is actually two major summits—the higher, more westerly summit of Batian (5,199 meters/ 17,058 feet) and the only slightly lower Nelion (5,188 meters/17,021 feet)— separated by a gap of 140 meters. There are also numerous other spires on the Mount Kenya massif, each with its own distinct characteristics.

In general, Mount Kenya's routes tend to be harder than those on Kilimanjaro, but a wide variety of climbs exists on both. Indeed, there are over a hundred documented routes of all difficulties on both the mountains.

This guidebook came about after I spent six weeks in Patagonia in 1995 with Charlie French, a British climber who had "done" Kilimanjaro and spoke to me of wild jungles, bizarre rock formations, magnificent vistas, and old-fashioned railroads crossing the desolate plains of East Africa. I was hooked, and immediately set out to learn all I could about the mountain, and the area. Unfortunately, few sources of information exist, and in the end, I decided that an up-to-date guidebook was in order.

This book covers all the major forest and moorland routes that lead to the main peaks on Kilimanjaro and Mount Kenya. I also describe the most popular routes to the summits of Kibo and Mawenzi on Kilimanjaro, and to Batian, Nelion, Point Lenana, and other summits on Mount Kenya. Greatest attention is given to the most popular routes, with decreasing amounts of information on less popular, more obscure ones. Some routes on both peaks have been omitted altogether because they are so rarely climbed and are of little interest to the majority of visiting climbers.

A selection of maps describes the areas around Kilimanjaro and Mount Kenya, as well as the forest and moorland approach routes to the main peaks. Technical mountaineering routes are covered both in verbal descriptions and with photographs and route overlays.

Because my aim was to help North American and European mountaineers understand the various requirements for entering Tanzania and Kenya, as well as those of Mount Kenya and Kilimanjaro National Parks, I have also included preliminary chapters on these topics. And since the crux of climbing in East Africa is getting to the mountains and dealing with everyday East African problems, there are sections on trip planning, transportation to and within East Africa, visa requirements, currency, health, and details important to the traveler. Useful addresses, a glossary of local languages, and a suggested reading list are given in appendixes at the end of the book.

Finally, this book is an attempt to persuade you, the visiting mountaineer, to keep these popular mountains clean. The high points of continents—the "seven summits," as they're commonly known—are being hammered. My own personal prediction is that all seven of the continental high points will, by the year 2010, have quotas on the numbers of climbers allowed to ascend them. Kilimanjaro already has a limit of fifty-eight nonresident visitors per day on the Marangu Route. The more garbage and human waste that park rangers have to pick up after us, the lower the quotas are likely to be.

Both Kilimanjaro and Mount Kenya are wild mountains in a wild part of the world. And both offer a route for every level of trekker and climber. Go, enjoy, climb, and learn again what it's like to be in awe.

Contact Cameron Burns, c/o The Mountaineers Books, 1001 SW Klickitat Way, Suite 201, Seattle, WA 98134, if you have any updates to information you would like to share for future reprints of this book.

A NOTE ABOUT SAFETY

Safety is an important concern in all outdoor activities. No guidebook can alert you to every hazard or anticipate the limitations of every reader. Therefore, the descriptions of roads, trails, routes, and natural features in this book are not representations that a particular place or excursion will be safe for your party. When you follow any of the routes described in this book, you assume responsibility for your own safety. Under normal conditions, such excursions require the usual attention to traffic, road and trail conditions, weather, terrain, the capabilities of your party, and other factors. Keeping informed on current conditions and exercising common sense are the keys to a safe, enjoyable outing.

—*The Mountaineers*

CHAPTER 1

HISTORY

...a vast mountain of gold and silver in the far interior, the approach to which was guarded by evil spirits.
—Johann Rebmann, after sighting Kilimanjaro
on May 11, 1848

The existence of high mountains in East Africa was known to Europeans as far back as the first century A.D., when a Greek merchant sighted "a snowy range of mountains" during a journey through inland Kenya. Ptolemy included these peaks on his early maps of Africa, placing them near the head of the Nile River.

In the sixteenth century, Spanish explorer Fernandez de Encisco wrote: "West of [Mombasa] stands the Ethiopian Mountain Olympus, which is exceeding high, and beyond it are the Mountains of the Moon, which are the sources of the Nile."

The mysterious mountains of East Africa—and the existence of snow near the equator—were a point of curiosity and controversy for European explorers for centuries.

KILIMANJARO

The mid-nineteenth century saw exploration of East Africa by European colonial powers eager for raw materials, agricultural lands, and slaves. While many sought wealth, a few—like London-based Church Missionary Society representatives Johann Rebmann and Dr. Ludwig Krapf—sought souls in need of saving.

In 1846, Rebmann and Krapf landed on the east coast of Africa and established a mission near Mombasa, where they heard tales of an enormous mountain lying in the interior. On May 11, 1848, while on a journey inland, Rebmann caught sight of Kilimanjaro from a point about a day's travel from Taveta. In his diary he wrote:

> *This morning, at ten o'clock, we obtained a clearer view of the mountains of Jagga, the summit of one of which was covered by what looked like a beautiful white cloud. When I inquired as to the dazzling whiteness, the guide merely called it "cold," and at once I knew it could be neither more nor less than snow. . . . I immediately understood how to interpret the marvelous tales Dr. Krapf and I had heard at the coast, of a vast mountain of gold and silver in the far interior, the approach to which was guarded by evil spirits.*

On a second expedition in November, Rebmann reached the village of Majamé (Machame), a point closer to Kilimanjaro than any other European had ever traveled, and was able to accurately describe the shape of the enormous mountain:

> *There are two main peaks, which arise from a common base measuring some twenty-five miles long by as many broad. They are separated by a saddle-shaped depression, running east and west for a distance of about eight or ten miles. The eastern peak is the lower of the two, and is conical in shape. The western and higher presents the appearance of a magnificent dome, and is covered with snow throughout the year, unlike its eastern neighbor which loses its snowy mantle during the hot season. By the Swahili at the coast, the mountain is known as Kilimanjaro (Mountain of Greatness) but the Wa-Jagga call it Kibo, from the snow with which it is perpetually capped.*

On a third expedition in early 1849, Rebmann again reached Majamé and, venturing toward Kilimanjaro, got "so close to the snowline that, supposing no impassable abyss to intervene, I could have reached it in three or four hours." Unfortunately he was too ill to continue the ascent.

In November 1849, Krapf made his own inland expedition. First visiting the Ukamba district, east of Kilimanjaro, he obtained "a magnificent view of the snow-mountain Kilimanjaro in Jagga, which loomed up from behind the ranges of Ndara and Bura. . . . Even at this distance

I could make out that the white substance crowning the summit was certainly snow." Krapf estimated Kilimanjaro's height at 3,810 meters (12,500 feet). He then continued on to Kitui, in what is today central Kenya, to make the first definitive recorded sighting of Mount Kenya by a European.

The Great Debate

"The reality of snow on these twin equatorial mountains, Kilimanjaro and Mount Kenya, was not at first accepted in London, and learned discussions took place on the subject before the Royal Geographical Society," wrote Halford John Mackinder, the explorer to make the first ascent of Mount Kenya. The argument was not over whether snow-clad peaks could exist at the equator, as scholars were already well aware of the high peaks of the Andes. The issue was whether these particular mountains in East Africa were tall enough to have snow.

In August 1861, German explorer Baron Von der Decken and English geologist R. Thornton attempted to climb Kilimanjaro and spent three days trying to penetrate the forest zone on the mountain's lower slopes. They were eventually forced back by bad weather, having reached only 2,500 meters.

In 1862, Von der Decken returned with Dr. Otto Kersten. Starting from Moji (Moshi) in December, the two became the first white men to climb beyond the forest zone, reaching a height of 4,300 meters. "During the night it snowed heavily," Von der Decken recorded in his journal, "and next morning the ground lay white all around us."

Von der Decken and Kersten estimated the height of Kibo at 5,700 meters (18,680 feet), its snowline at 4,998 meters, and its vegetation line at 3,657 meters. They estimated Mawenzi at a height of 4,953 meters (16,250 feet). Their findings ended, for the most part, the intense debate.

First Attempts

The flood of Kilimanjaro exploration and first-ascent attempts that followed Von der Decken and Kersten came partially as a result of the struggle between the East African colonial powers to turn the findings of the continent's explorers into material gain.

By the early 1880s, a railroad was under construction across the central portion of Tanzania from Dar es Salaam to Ujiji on Lake Tanganyika, and to travelers on the completed portions of this line, Kilimanjaro had become a familiar sight to the north.

Lying close to the coast and to overland routes to Lake Tanganyika, Kilimanjaro saw several attempts at ascent in the early 1880s, mostly by missionaries and government officials.

By the late 1880s, ascents to the saddle between Kibo and Mawenzi were commonplace, and the village of Marangu was generally accepted as the best starting place for attempts on Kilimanjaro, as it was the highest point on the mountain that could easily be reached.

First Ascent: Hans Meyer

Following advice from the Austro-Hungarian team of Count Samuel Teleki and Lieutenant Ludwig von Holnel, who had reached 4,815 meters on the mountain, Hans Meyer, a leading German geographer of the day, and his companion, Herr von Eberstein, began an ascent of Kilimanjaro in August 1887. Climbing to the Saddle, they reached an altitude of 5,486 meters on Kibo, probably the highest any European had ascended to date. "Here, further progress was checked by the precipitous face of the ice cap, and we were compelled to turn back," Meyer later wrote.

In the fall of 1888, Otto Ehlers, a representative of the German East Africa Company, attempted the peak with a Dr. Abbott, an American naturalist. Ehlers would be the first European to assert he had reached Kibo's summit—a claim he later rescinded.

After pitching camp at 2,987 meters, Ehlers set off alone for Mawenzi, reaching an altitude of 4,998 meters. He and Abbott then shifted camp to the foot of Kibo. The next morning they began an ascent of Kibo, but at around 5,181 meters, Abbott became ill and returned to camp.

At around 10:00 A.M., Ehlers reached "the wall of ice which encircles the entire summit." After a few more hours spent searching for a way through the ice, Ehlers wrote, he "succeeded in reaching the northwestern side of the summit and gained a tolerably extensive view of the surroundings."

Ehlers's ascent was widely questioned, and he later admitted that there was a point on the crater rim south of the spot he reached that appeared to be 60 meters higher, and that he had probably been mistaken that the point he had reached was the summit.

With Europeans wandering all over Kilimanjaro, Meyer knew the prize of the first ascent wouldn't last long, and in the northern summer of 1889, he put together a second expedition to Kilimanjaro with Ludwig Purtscheller. From Mombasa, the expedition—which included sixty-five porters—traveled to Marangu. There, Meyer assembled a smaller team of porters that would attempt the mountain and also made arrangements for an intermediate camp between Marangu and the saddle area, to be restocked with food by Marangu porters every few days.

Meyer's team departed Marangu on September 28 with nine porters, two headmen, two guides, and several cooks. On October 2, after several days' travel through the forest, they reached 4,328 meters, camping about 2.4 kilometers from the foot of Kibo. As they examined the peak that evening, Meyer and Purtscheller decided to attempt a route that climbed a prominent ravine, then ascended the Ratzel Glacier.

Leaving camp at 2:30 A.M., they toiled for several hours on the gravelly lower slopes of Kibo and by 7:00 A.M. reached an altitude of 4,998 meters and "the first flakes of snow."

"Every ten minutes we had to pause a few seconds to give heart and lungs a rest, for we were now far above the height of Mount Blanc," Meyer later wrote, "and the increasing rarity of the atmosphere made itself more and more painfully felt."

At the base of the Ratzel Glacier, Purtscheller donned his crampons. Meyer, who had none, had to trust his hobnailed boots. Chopping steps up the glacier was a formidable task, and every step took "some twenty strokes of the axe."

In all, they took about 3 hours to climb the glacier and by 2:00 P.M. had reached the crater rim. "A few more steps in eager anticipation and the secret of Kibo lay unveiled before us—at our feet yawned a gigantic crater, with precipitous walls, occupying the entire summit of the mountain," Meyer wrote.

They decided against continuing on to the true summit, which appeared to be at least an hour and a half away, and descended the route by which they had come, rechopping steps in the glacier and struggling into camp just before 7:00 P.M.

The next day, Meyer moved camp closer to the base of Kibo, and after a night's rest he and Purtscheller began another ascent on October 5. "At a quarter to nine, we reached our old point on the crater rim at an altitude of 19,200 feet [5,852 meters]," he wrote, "but almost immediately pushed on again, all eager to reach our little outstanding pinnacle on the southern side, on which our hearts were set."

The pair walked around the crater rim, scaling three small "rocky pinnacles" in a "leisurely and systematic fashion" before Meyer took an aneroid reading and found the central pinnacle "attained an altitude of 19,700 feet [6,004 meters], overtopping the others by some forty or fifty feet." The happy climbers congratulated each other, and Meyer planted a small German flag in the volcanic debris of Kibo's summit, which they named Kaiser Wilhelm Spitze (Kaiser Wilhelm Peak) in honor of their king.

They made several sketches of the crater, then returned by way of the Ratzel Glacier to their high camp.

On October 13, Meyer and Purtscheller made a bold attempt to climb Mawenzi (also known then as Kibwezi) but were defeated by loose rock and difficult routefinding. On October 15, they attempted the mountain again but accidentally climbed Klute Peak (5,095 meters/ 16,716 feet), one of Mawenzi's many subsidiary summits. On October 21, they made a third attempt on Mawenzi but were again thwarted in reaching the main summit (5,149 meters/16,893 feet).

The remainder of Meyer's now famous "ten days above fifteen thousand feet"—the title of a chapter in his book describing the first ascent of Kilimanjaro—were spent attempting Kibo from the north. Several more attempts resulted in their reaching Kibo's crater, which they wandered around inside, but they did not, however, regain the summit.

Meyer's original name for the highest point of Kibo, Kaiser Wilhelm Spitze, still appears on some maps of Kilimanjaro.

Kilimanjaro, 1890–1930

It was a decade before Kibo was climbed again. In 1898, Meyer returned with E. Platz and climbed Kibo to the crater rim. In October of the same year, Captain Johannes Korner climbed a route close to today's Normal Route, as far as Gillman's Point. Like many people who made ascents to the crater rim in the following years, Korner did not continue on to the true summit.

In July 1909, a surveyor, M. Lange, and his assistant, a man named Weigele, climbed the Normal Route to the crater rim via Johannes Notch, then continued to the summit of Kibo, making what is generally accepted as the second ascent of the mountain and the first ascent of the Normal Route.

In 1912, the summit of Mawenzi was claimed for the first time— like Kibo, by German climbers. On June 29, Fritz Klute and Edward Oehler made the first ascent of Hans Meyer Peak (5,149 meters/16,893 feet), the tallest point on Mawenzi. They then climbed Kibo from the west, via the Upper Drygalski Glacier, and descended via the Great Western Arch (the Western Breach Route).

Klute and Oehler were followed a few months later by German climbers Walter Furtwangler and Ziegfried Koenig, who reached the summit of Kibo (on skis) for its fourth ascent, and that of Hans Meyer Peak for Mawenzi's second ascent. Two more ascents of Kibo were made before World War I, as well as the first ascent of Gillman's Point by a woman, Frau von Ruckteschell, a German.

Mawenzi

After World War I, Mawenzi became a focus for many climbers, mostly because so little was known about the impressive peak.

In 1924, George Londt of the Mountain Club of South Africa and a local guide named Offoro attempted to climb Hans Meyer Peak but miscalculated and made the first ascent of South Peak (4,958 meters/ 16,266 feet) (now Londt Peak).

On July 28, 1927, English climbers William West, Otho Brown, and the first woman to climb Mawenzi, Sheila MacDonald, made the third ascent of Hans Meyer Peak, by a variation of the original route. A few days later, MacDonald went on to become the first woman to climb Kibo to Kaiser Wilhelm Spitze.

Also of note during these early years was an ascent of Mawenzi in March 1930 by the highly talented British team of Eric Shipton and Bill Tilman. After climbing Kibo, the pair made an ascent of a couloir running northwest of the west face, which Shipton correctly believed to be the Oehler Gully. At the top of the gully, Shipton and Tilman went left, instead of right, and climbed Nordecke Peak (5,140 meters/16,863 feet). "I think the mistake gave us a first ascent," Shipton later wrote. They then descended and climbed Hans Meyer Peak.

In 1932, Kibo Hut was built, and hotels in Marangu began operating guided ascents of Kilimanjaro for tourists.

By the early 1960s, climbing Kilimanjaro had become a "popular business...one must expect competition from all ages and sexes, from middle aged ladies to 12-year-old boys," observed F. R. Brooke in the *Alpine Journal*. The journal also recorded that in 1959 more than seven hundred people attempted Kilimanjaro, but only about half that number reached Gillman's Point.

The first half of the twentieth century also saw the beginning of exploration of the southern glaciers, with the first ascent of the Decken Glacier by E. Eisenmann and T. Schnackig on January 12, 1938. First ascents of the Kersten and Heim Glaciers followed in the 1950s.

The 1970s brought perhaps the greatest period of new routing in Kilimanjaro's history, when climbers like Iain Allan, Ian Howell, Mark

Savage, Bill O'Connor, John Cleare, Dave Cheesmond, and John Temple explored new lines and variations on the existing glacier routes.

By the late 1970s, the one prize that still awaited climbers was the Breach Wall, a 1,400-meter precipice containing two steep glaciers separated by hundreds of meters of vertical ice. In 1977 and 1978, two teams—one British, the other American—attempted the wall unsuccessfully.

In January 1978, Reinhold Messner and Konrad Renzler attempted "the Breach," and, following two prominent icefalls directly up the wall, climbed the route in an astonishing 12 hours. Messner later called it "the most dangerous wall I have ever climbed."

MOUNT KENYA

Although by the early 1880s, Kilimanjaro was the subject of much exploration, the existence of Mount Kenya was still being questioned by many explorers and geographers.

In 1883, the Geographical Society sent Scottish explorer Joseph Thomson to investigate. Beginning at the coast and traveling inland, Thomson passed Kilimanjaro, found the elusive Mount Kenya, and even made an attempt on the peak that reached 2,743 meters. In his 1885 report of the trip, he suggested that the mountain was an extinct volcano.

First Ascent: Halford John Mackinder

After unsuccessfully attempting Kilimanjaro in 1887, Count Teleki attempted to climb Mount Kenya from the southwest. However, although he managed to reach the upper portion of the mountain and a height of 4,350 meters, the summit eluded him.

Several years later, a group of British East Africa Company officials under the command of Captain F. G. Dundas attempted the mountain from the south but failed to even penetrate the forest surrounding the main peaks.

In 1893, John W. Gregory, a British geologist, managed to climb to 4,730 meters—remarkably, since he had no climbing equipment and was suffering from fever.

Gregory was followed in 1894 and 1896 by George Kolb, a German physician who pioneered a route through the forests on the east side of the mountain but failed to reach the main peaks. Ironically, Kolb's badly supplied expeditions became a model of "what not to do" for Halford Mackinder, the first person to summit Mount Kenya.

Born in 1861 in Lincolnshire, England, Halford John Mackinder was a scholar whose life revolved primarily around academia and science. He was familiar with the exploration of East Africa during the latter half of the century, as well as the various reports of a great mountain mass in the central part of the British East African Protectorate, as Kenya was then known, and in 1899 put together an expedition to attempt an ascent of the mysterious mountain.

In June 1899, Mackinder set sail for Africa with Campbell Hausberg, Douglas Saunders, César Ollier, and Joseph Brocherel. Riding the newly built inland train from Mombasa, they arrived in Nairobi on July 15. After some negotiations and the hiring of porters and guides, the party struck out across the Kapoti Plains north of Nairobi on July 28.

"All told, we were 170 strong," Mackinder wrote in the *Geographical Journal*. "Six Europeans, 66 Swahilis, two tall Masai guides, and the remainder were naked Kikuyu."

It is remarkable that Mackinder's expedition ever made it to Mount Kenya, let alone managed to climb the mountain. Throughout the month-long approach march, the guides and porters regularly became ill; they took food and women from the local villages through which they passed, angering the local people; they stole provisions from the expedition itself; and they deserted Mackinder at every turn. Additionally, the local chiefs were at times extremely hostile and killed dozens of Mackinder's men.

Amazingly, by August 18, Mackinder had reached the foot of the mountain and set up a base camp in the forest east of the main peaks. From this point, the climbing party was trimmed down to twelve "volunteers" who would stay on the mountain with Mackinder, and forty-two porters and Kikuyus who would carry loads to a high camp.

Mackinder approached the mountain following the Hohnel Valley, and made his high camp, Camp XXII, at around 3,140 meters in the upper Teleki Valley.

On August 30, Mackinder, Ollier, and Brocherel attempted an ascent of the peak via the south face of Nelion. They came very close to making the first ascent of Nelion but—after a cold night out just below the summit—retreated in the morning.

On September 5, Hausberg, Ollier, and Brocherel made a circuit of the main peaks, climbing Point Lenana (4,985 meters/16,355 feet) in the process.

On September 11, Ollier and Brocherel attempted to climb the peak via the Darwin Glacier but were turned back by bad weather.

Finally, on September 12, Mackinder, Ollier, and Brocherel started up the mountain yet again, climbing the south face of Nelion to the crest of the South Ridge. After spending the night in a Mummery tent (an oversized bivouac sack that used ice axes as poles) amongst the rocks on the ridge crest, the trio descended to the Upper Darwin Glacier, then traversed Nelion and across the top of the Diamond Glacier into the Gate of the Mists.

"It took three hours to cut our way across the hanging glacier to the further side of the gap between the two summits," Mackinder later wrote. "The glacier was steep, so that our shoulders were close to it. Had we fallen, we should have gone over an ice cliff onto the [Lower] Darwin Glacier several hundred feet below."

A short scramble led to the summit of Batian (5,199 meters/17,058 feet), where the climbers celebrated and took photographs. They retraced their route to the Lewis Glacier, then to Camp XXII, which they reached at 10:30 P.M., "hungry and weary, but triumphant."

Mount Kenya, 1900–1930

After Mackinder's successful ascent, there were many exploratory expeditions to Mount Kenya in the first two decades of the twentieth century, but none of these was successful in reaching the summit.

Then, at the end of the 1920s, famed British mountaineer Eric Shipton teamed up with various partners to climb several new routes on both the main peaks and made first ascents of many of the subsidiary summits.

On January 3, 1929, Shipton and fellow Briton Percy Wyn Harris made the first ascent of Nelion via the modern Normal Route. Descending into the Gate of the Mists, they then climbed Batian, making the second overall ascent of the mountain. The climb was repeated on January 8 by Shipton, Harris, and Norwegian climber Gustav Sommerfelt.

The Normal Route was repeated a third time in December 1929 by Shipton and Pat Russell; the pair then went on to make the first ascent of Point John (4,883 meters/16,020 feet).

In July 1930, Shipton returned to Mount Kenya with Bill Tilman. The two began an extensive reconnaissance of Batian and Nelion, during which they made the first ascents of Point Dutton (4,885 meters/16,207 feet—then known as Dutton Peak) and Point Peter (4,757 meters/15,607 feet).

On August 1, Shipton and Tilman made the first ascent of the West Ridge of Batian, climbing the route in one long day from Firmin Col.

This ascent was also the first traverse of the mountain, as the descent was made down the Normal Route. On August 5, the pair climbed Sendeyo (4,704 meters/15,433 feet), and the next day made the first ascent of Point Pigott (4,957 meters/16,263 feet), via the northwest face. On August 9, they made the first ascent of Midget Peak (4,700 meters/ 15,420 feet), climbing the south gully.

The few years before World War II saw relatively little activity. The highlights of the period included the first ascents of both Nelion and Batian by women. In February 1938, Miss C. Carol reached the summit of Nelion with Mtu Muthara, the first African to climb that peak. And in March of 1938, Miss Una Cameron became the first woman to climb Batian.

The North Face

By the early 1940s, ascents of Batian and Nelion via the Normal Route were becoming commonplace, and all serious mountaineers had their eyes on the north face of Batian.

"The war and postwar periods brought to Kenya a large number of Europeans, amongst whom were some keen mountaineers," observed Mount Kenya historian John W. Howard in 1953.

The leading pioneer of this period was undoubtedly Arthur Firmin, who succeeded on several new, important routes and in the period between 1943 and 1950 climbed Batian five times, by every existing route except the west face.

In early 1944, Firmin and two fellow Brits reached a height of 4,907 meters on the north face. In July, Firmin returned and with fellow Briton P. H. Hicks managed to climb the North Face Route in just a morning, reaching the summit of Batian at 1:30 P.M.

In January 1946, Firmin and John W. Howard climbed the Southwest Ridge, calling it "one of the shortest and most direct routes to the top of Batian." And, finally, in 1950, Firmin and John S. Bagenal climbed the Darwin and Diamond Glaciers, thus creating the South Face Route. It was the second time—after Mackinder—that the Diamond Glacier had been traversed.

In 1952, two French climbers, Maurice Martin and Roger Rangaux, climbed a route on the northeast face, 100 meters left of the Firmin-Hicks (North Face Standard) Route.

In January 1955, R. A. Caukwell and G. W. Rose made the first ascent of the west face of Batian, joining the West Ridge not far below the summit of Batian. Unfortunately, Rose was badly injured and knocked unconscious while the pair were descending the Normal Route on Nelion. Upon reaching the Lewis Glacier, Caukwell ran 32 kilometers down the mountain to summon help, but by the time he returned with a rescue party, Rose was dead. Because of the hazards that might be created in lowering the body, Rose was left—for a time—on Nelion's southeast face.

Shortly after Rose and Caukwell's climb, Howard calculated that by January 1955, Batian had been climbed nineteen times and Nelion thirty.

In January 1959, Kisoi Munyao became the first African to climb Batian, making the ascent with Howard and Peter Fullerton. During the same month, John Graham, a sixty-three-year-old American from California, climbed Batian with two Zermatt guides.

In February 1959, the Northey Glacier Route was climbed by W. M. Adams and Robert Chambers of the Mountain Club of Kenya. The pair took 9.5 hours to reach the summit of Batian from a bivouac at the foot of the Northey Glacier. Adams returned in August and climbed the North Chimney variation of the French Route with A. Bennett.

In October 1959, the Mountain Club of Kenya produced its first guidebook to Kilimanjaro and Mount Kenya, under the editorial direction of Ian Reid.

In January 1961, a "strong" party from the University of Cape Town visited Mount Kenya and climbed several new routes. On January 4, Robert "Rusty" Baillie and R. M. Kamke made the first ascent of the Southern Slabs Route, left of the Diamond Couloir, in 10 hours. Next, Baillie and Chris Rhys-Jones climbed a variation of the South Face Route. Instead of finishing by ascending Batian, the pair then climbed the south face of Nelion.

The East Face
By the early 1960s, interest had shifted to the east face of Mount Kenya. In 1953, John W. Howard observed:

> The only face of the mountain that has not yet been climbed is the east or northeast face which looks towards Simba Col. It is a tremendous jumble of precipices, buttresses and organ pipe columns; if Shipton and Wyn Harris could not find a gap in these defenses, then anybody who succeeds without the use of ironmongery (and probably with it, too) will have something to be proud of.

Kenyan climber Barry Cliff was the pioneer in east-face routes. In August 1963, Cliff and Denis Rutowitz decided to try the northeast face. First, the pair made the second ascent of the 1952 French Route so they could examine the pillar left of the route. Then, on August 2, they began climbing "the last great problem on Mount Kenya." "Unexpectedly, the rock was firm, much better than on any other part of the mountain," Cliff later wrote, "and here also there were odd little alpine flowers growing in the eastern facing corners." After two bivouacs on the wall (one below the Grey Pillar, the second above), the two men summitted on August 4, at about 1:30 P.M., then rappelled their route. The climb is now known as the Northeast Pillar of Nelion.

A few days later, Cliff was at it again, this time with Austrian climbers Heinrich Klier and Siegfried Aeberli. On August 7, the trio climbed the East Face Route, a series of cracks that runs from the summit all the way to the Krapf Glacier.

In March 1964, Baillie returned to Mount Kenya and with Tom Phillips made the first "Grand Traverse" of the mountain, climbing the South Ridge of Point Pigott, descending to Firmin Col, making the third ascent of the West Ridge to Batian, then crossing the Gate of the Mists to Nelion before descending the entire South Ridge of Nelion to Point John. The pair had two bivouacs. Baillie and Phillips also climbed a new route on Point John, then hauled up the materials to construct "Baillie's Bivy" near Mackinder's Gendarme on Nelion's Normal Route.

The 1970s saw something of a new-route explosion on Mount Kenya, as not only the hardest rock routes were tackled, but nearly all the major ice routes were climbed for the first time.

Nairobi-based climbers Ian Howell and Iain Allan undoubtedly led the pack in new routing, but many other climbers were involved during this period, including Roger Higgins, Phil Snyder, Mark Savage, John Temple, T. Mathenge, Y. Laulan, and B. LeDain. The massive record of new routes produced during the 1970s is too long to list here; suffice to say that all the major lines on Mount Kenya were climbed by the end of the decade.

The first ascent of the Diamond Couloir is noteworthy, because it was accomplished over a five-year period as various parties climbed portions of the route. In 1971, Howell and Snyder climbed the couloir to the bottom of the Diamond Glacier, at which point "the climb was virtually over" before the lateness of the day prompted the pair to rappel down the couloir to camp. In 1973, Snyder returned with Mathenge and climbed the entire route. Then, in 1975, Yvon Chouinard and Michael Covington climbed the steepest portion of the headwall below the Diamond Glacier, the route many parties now take. In 1977, Hillary Collins became the first woman to make the ascent of the Diamond Couloir.

By the early 1980s, all the major lines on Mount Kenya had been climbed, and ascents of new routes has slowed to a trickle. In 1989, Polish climbers Krzysztof Gwozdz and Zbyszek Wach added a new route on the Diamond Buttress, called Diamond Natasha, which crosses Southern Slabs before ascending a series of cracks between Southern Slabs and the Diamond Buttress Original Route. In 1992, British climbers Andrew Wielochowski and Chris Mockett pioneered a route on the north side of Nelion's South Ridge, while Brits Pat Littlejohn and John Mothersele climbed a new route on Point John's overhanging west face.

Future climbers to the mountain are likely to find little in the way of new routes to be done, and, as in other mountaineering arenas of the world, will likely focus on speed ascents and variations.

CHAPTER 2

ABOUT EAST AFRICA

GETTING THERE

General travel in East Africa is a topic far too broad to be covered in this guidebook. However, when it comes to getting to Kilimanjaro and Mount Kenya, the information you need to know is fairly brief.

For climbers heading to East Africa, there is really only one destination: Nairobi, or, as writer Geoff Crowther refers to the place in his travel guides, "Nairobbery." Certainly Nairobi has a crime problem, but it's no worse than you'd find in any city in North America or Europe. Be warned, though: don't go out after dark unless it's in a taxi!

Getting to Nairobi by air from Europe or America is fairly simple. There are no American airlines that fly to Africa directly or indirectly; however, several excellent European airlines fly there several times per week.

The most reliable and frequent services are offered by Lufthansa, KLM, and British Airways. Lufthansa offers Nairobi service from Europe and North America via a connection in Frankfurt. KLM offers Nairobi service via Amsterdam, and British Airways via London. KLM even offers service direct from Europe to Kilimanjaro International Airport (KIA), which is 64 kilometers west of Moshi on the Arusha–Moshi Road. Although all three airlines offer service to Nairobi, Lufthansa and KLM seem to be better represented in East Africa.

Another option for climbers heading for Kilimanjaro is Dar es Salaam. "Dar," as it's more commonly known, is also served by the big-three airlines, plus many lesser-known ones. It also has a port, so you can sail there, if you have the time and the patience.

Dar seems to have a crime problem equivalent to Nairobi's. One

Canadian I heard about decided to go jogging in Dar in the afternoon. The hotel staff urged him not to; he insisted. He returned to his hotel several hours later completely naked. Muggers had stolen his wallet, his shoes, and all his clothing.

When it comes to price, getting to East Africa will be the single most expensive part of your trip. From North America, you can expect to pay anywhere between US$1,200 and $1,800 round trip, depending on the length of your stay and the season. From Europe, tickets range from about US$500 to $1,000.

When you get to your international carrier, ask for one of their huge plastic bags designed to protect backpacks in the airport's luggage system. The bags distributed by domestic airlines in North America are very thin and basically worthless. The European airlines (Lufthansa, KLM) make great plastic bags—so good, in fact, that I keep my pack in one the entire time I'm in East Africa. At night on the mountains, the bag is excellent for keeping out dew.

Nairobi

Nairobi is a large, modern city of about 2 million inhabitants. The downtown area is fairly compact, though, and it's easy to get around on foot.

Nairobi has all the services you could ever want or need, from five-star hotels to YMCAs, and from the latest big-screen films to upscale boutiques.

Upon your arrival at the airport, you'll be besieged by eager taxi drivers. Since there are no hotels anywhere near the airport and most international flights arrive late at night, you'll need to take a cab into town to a hotel. The ride should cost between 800 and 1,000 Kenyan shillings (Ksh), or about US$16 to $20. (For more on Kenyan and Tanzanian currency, see Currency, below.)

During daylight hours, there is bus service from the airport into Nairobi, leaving from between Unit 1 and Unit 2 in the departures area. The ride costs Ksh 20 (US$.50). However, I cannot recommend the bus, even for budget travelers—most tourists get their pockets picked on it. I did.

Many travelers on their first visit to Nairobi take a taxi straight to one of the various hotels on Harry Thuku Road in the University district. The hotels here are quiet, high-quality, and, most important, just a short walk from the Davanu shuttle depot. (For more on the Davanu shuttle, see Getting to the Mountains in Chapter 3.) There are many low-budget hotels in Nairobi, but if it's your first trip to Africa, staying in a nice place on your first night is a good idea.

Most of the cheaper hotels are located on the east side of town, between Tom Mboya Street and River Road. The YMCA is on State House Road, and the YWCA is on Mamlaka Road. You can stay at these places for around US$10 a night if they're not full. (For more on Nairobi hotels, see Appendix A.)

Most hotels in Nairobi will store your extra baggage for free, or a small fee. Faxing a reservation from the United States or Europe is highly recommended for your first night.

As far as restaurants go, there are hundreds of good places to dine, and you'll soon find that Nairobi has exceptional Indian and Middle Eastern food.

One place that many climbers head for is Carnivore. At this unique restaurant, meat of all sorts—including zebra, crocodile, waterbuck, hartebeest, giraffe, and various gazelles—are grilled over an open pit on Masai spears. Waiters wander around the place with huge *pangas* (machetes), carving off as much meat as you want. Dinner is about US$25, but the taxi ride will cost you another US$12 or so each way. An even better experience—if you like to mix with the locals—is a *nyama choma,* or barbecue place. There are many, and they are much cheaper than Carnivore, but you'll be eating domestic meat rather than game.

Airport Departure Tax and Value Added Tax

Kenya and Tanzania both require an airport departure tax each time you leave the country, payable either in local currency or U.S. dollars. In 1997, the tax was US$20 in both countries, but it could—and probably will—go up at any time.

East African nations tack on an extra 15 percent government tax—the Value Added Tax (V.A.T.)—to most goods and services. This tax will be included in most of your bills, but occasionally you will see "V.A.T." at the bottom of a bill, with the actual dollar or shilling amount of the tax.

GETTING ALONG

Whereas most European mountaineers and trekkers are generally familiar with East African society because historical ties are strong and the area is relatively close, North Americans are fairly naive about life in East Africa.

Kenya and Tanzania are developing nations, and travelers must be prepared to deal with all the problems such countries experience. Many things we take for granted in Western nations simply don't apply in

Africa. Vehicles break down with alarming regularity. The telephone system is prehistoric. People drive like maniacs. Appointments can occur days late. And the water can be bad.

But for all those problems, East Africa is a magical place, and the people who live there are incredibly friendly. Often, traveling throughout the region, you might be taken aback by the serious stares you'll get from the local people. They are just checking you out, trying to figure out what you're all about. Crack a smile, and instantly an East African's face will go from serious to smiling.

Also, if you are going to climb both Kilimanjaro and Mount Kenya, you'll notice a difference between Tanzanians and Kenyans. Tanzanians tend to be much more outgoing; Kenyans are more serious and more reserved.

Wages and Tips

Some of the richest and poorest people in the world live in East Africa. However, by North American and European standards, the average person is dirt poor.

The average monthly wage of a gardener or laborer in Tanzania is about 18,000 Tanzanian shillings (Tsh)(about US$36); a car or truck driver makes about Tsh 20,000 (about US$40); a security guard, around Tsh 30,000 (about US$60). Wages in Kenya are comparable. The average monthly wage of a waiter in a small town is about Ksh 1,200 (about US$24), excluding tips.

East Africans work incredibly hard. The waiter who makes US$24 a month may work from 7:00 A.M. to midnight every day. Because of their low wages, people who serve you hope that good service will be rewarded with a tip. I generally overtip wildly (sometimes as much as 30 percent for really good, cheerful service), but 10 to 15 percent is the standard.

Language

The predominant languages in East Africa are Kiswahili, more commonly known in the Western world as Swahili, and English. Most East Africans grow up learning their tribal "mother tongue" first. Swahili and English come later. Fortunately for travelers, nearly everyone in Kenya and Tanzania has some working knowledge of English, and many speak English very well. Beyond English, the more common European languages (French, German, Spanish) are virtually unknown.

While Swahili is the predominant language in the Kilimanjaro area, in the area around Mount Kenya, locals still prefer to speak in their tribal languages. On the east side of the mountain, the tribal language is Meru. On the west, it's Kikuyu. In Appendix B are Swahili, Kikuyu, and Meru translations for words commonly used in mountaineering.

Food

For the gourmet, East Africa will be something of a disappointment. Cooked dishes tend to be fried, deep-fried, or boiled meat with some starchy food like potatoes or rice, and everything seems to have a double shot of grease. Even on Kili, where your meals are prepared by local cooks, most of the food is deep-fried or boiled.

One staple you'll run into is *ugali,* a type of cornmeal often served with meat. On its own it's extremely bland, but soaking up the juice from a stew, it's delicious.

On the other hand, the uncooked fruits and vegetables are superb, especially the fruit. Just be sure to peel all fruits and vegetables before eating raw.

If you're a vegetarian, good luck. I went on a camel safari in Kenya where the vegetarians were fed plain white rice and plain cabbage.

Alcohol

There are numerous brands of excellent local beers available in Kenya and Tanzania. They come in 500-milliliter bottles, so if you normally like a couple of beers after climbing a mountain, you might need only one of these. In Kenya, Tusker and Pilsner are the most prevalent brands. Kenbrew, Citizen, and Castle (from South Africa) are also common. In Tanzania, the most common beer is Safari Lager.

Besides beers, there are several locally made spirits that are worth a try. Kenya Cane (in Kenya) and Konyagi (in Tanzania) are distilled from sugarcane and actually taste fairly good.

If you want a wild experience after getting down off Kilimanjaro, ask your driver to stop for some banana beer. This stuff is served in 2-liter plastic buckets and is made of ground-up, half-fermented bananas. It costs about Tsh 50 (US$.10) a bucket.

In Kenya, you might be offered some *changaa.* This pungent liquor is distilled from vegetable scraps and tastes like it. A liter is only a hundred Kenyan shillings, but it's so foul you'll want to skip it altogether.

One thing to watch out for: East African beer bottles splinter easily. When you or your waiter pops the top, keep an eye out for slivers cracking off around the rim. If it happens, don't drink the beer! Ask for another.

Currency

The currency in both Tanzania and Kenya is based on the shilling. Amounts are written with a prefix of "Tsh" (Tanzanian shillings) or "Ksh" (Kenyan shillings). As of late 1998, the exchange rate was about Tsh 660 or Ksh 61 to the U.S. dollar.

Traveler's checks and foreign currency can be exchanged at most banks or at Forex Bureaus, government-approved currency exchanges that can be found in most towns throughout Tanzania and Kenya.

If you use traveler's checks, VISA ones are far more widely accepted in East Africa than any other type. I've seen people with American Express traveler's checks turned down when trying to cash them. Also, a few picky Forex Bureaus won't cash traveler's checks unless you have the receipts showing that you purchased them. Those are the same receipts you normally keep separate from the checks themselves in case you are robbed, so make an extra set. Most banks will cash your traveler's checks without any problems.

In Kenya, credit cards are widely accepted. VISA cards are the most commonly accepted ones. Make sure that when you go to Africa your credit card is new and that the magnetic strip is in good condition. Many East African business owners/operators are still fairly ignorant about credit card charging, and if their card reader can't read your magnetic strip, they won't let you charge anything.

When you get to Tanzania, you can put your credit card away. Almost no one accepts them. Some Tanzanian banks won't let you draw cash on a credit card as they do in Kenya, and ones that do charge about 30 percent commission. Businesses that accept credit cards of any kind are few and far between.

Kenya is starting to see ATMs (automatic teller machines) go up everywhere. As in the rest of the world, these machines accept credit cards and are a good way to buy the local currency. There is an ATM in the arrivals building at Jomo Kenyatta International Airport in Nairobi that dispenses Kenyan currency. There's also one in Meru, at the Barclays Bank.

When you go out into the country (to Moshi for Kilimanjaro, or to any of the small towns surrounding Mount Kenya), bring lots of small change. Many hoteliers, restaurateurs, shop owners, and taxi drivers will claim they have no change when you hand them the equivalent of a $20 bill for a $5 product or service. Indeed, among my friends we have a saying: "There is no change in East Africa." I've learned that if you really start making a fuss, they'll find some change somewhere.

Besides money for park fees and guides or porters while climbing the mountain and transportation around Tanzania and Kenya, I always try to bring the equivalent of US$500 for emergencies, souvenir shopping, and general fun, although US$200 to $300 is plenty if you're on a budget.

In Tanzania, I never bring notes bigger than Tsh 10,000, and I try to get the majority of my cash converted into Tsh 1,000 notes. In Kenya, I never bring notes bigger than Ksh 1,000, and usually I try to get the majority of my cash converted into Ksh 500 or Ksh 200 notes.

If for some reason you forget to get your money exchanged before heading off to the mountains, don't worry. U.S. currency is widely accepted in East Africa, especially Tanzania, where U.S. dollars are often preferred over Tanzanian shillings.

Bank hours are generally 8:30 A.M. to 3:30 P.M. daily, and some even close at 12:30 P.M.

Telephones

Making a phone call is one of the most frustrating things you'll ever do in East Africa. Although many hotels have telephones you can use, the charge is enormous, partly because the tax on private phones is high. Expect to pay about US$20 to $30 for a 3-minute call to the United States, slightly less for Europe.

There are many telecommunications centers in East African towns that offer far more reasonable rates, sometimes as low as $6 for a 3-minute call. You can also fax from most telecommunications centers for about the same price.

Calling to East Africa is fairly simple. The country code for Tanzania is 255; for Kenya, 254. To dial direct from the United States, dial 011 for an international line, then the country code, followed by the number. Remember that East Africa is 8 to 11 hours ahead of the United States.

Also, don't be surprised if some people don't return your calls from East Africa. The price of a single phone call is a month's wages for the average person, so many East Africans are reluctant to phone internationally unless it's absolutely necessary. Most climbing outfitters and hotels will fax you back a confirmation of a booking when you make one.

Choos and *Pangas*

This might seem like a silly topic to write about, but a *choo* (Swahili for "toilet," pronounced *"chaw"*) in Africa is different from anything most

Americans will experience at home. Generally, nice hotels and restaurants have flush toilets with seats. However, the less expensive the place, the more likely it won't have a seat, or a bowl at all. In many places, the toilets are nothing more than a room with a hole in the floor.

Likewise, the *panga* (Swahili for "machete") is another East African speciality. In Tanzania and Kenya, everyone carries a *panga*. Some are huge, reminiscent of pirate swords; others are small and hooked. Don't feel threatened by someone holding a *panga*. Get used to them. Like a cold Tusker or Safari beer, *panga*s will become a constant in your life.

Film and Photography

In general, pretty much all the latest types of films, batteries, and videotape are available in the modern camera shops in Nairobi and Dar. Once you get out in the country, however, finding a roll of anything but color print film is difficult.

Moshi has an excellent camera shop called Kotty's, located near the bus station on Mawenzi Road. Kotty, a professional photographer, has all sorts of camera batteries and film, but prices are about double what you'd expect in the United States.

Nanyuki, on the north side of Mount Kenya, has a couple of good photo shops, and most of the bigger towns around Mount Kenya (Chogoria, Meru, Embu) have photo shops, although slide film is almost impossible to get.

When you're in East Africa, always ask your subject for permission before taking a photograph. You might have to pay a small fee, but it's considered the polite way to take a photograph. If you don't ask first, you might find yourself arguing with locals who want a small modeling fee.

It's important in Tanzania that you don't photograph any buildings, people, or offices associated with the government. Because of its political history, the Tanzanian government is still fairly paranoid about its relationships with other countries, and taking photos of any government facility could land you in jail.

AVOIDING RIP-OFFS

"Kenya is a nation of opportunists."

That is how a high-ranking Kenyan government official summed up the East African attitude toward business, tourism, and crime during an interview I conducted in 1997.

Although most Kenyans and Tanzanians are honest, hard-working people, many are looking to make a buck by cutting corners in tourism, overcharging for products and services, and straightforward pilfering. I can't tell you how many pocketknives I've had disappear while on Kilimanjaro.

The rip-offs are simple and complex. Some are legal, some are not. Following are a few of the more prevalent ones to watch out for.

Pickpockets

Although taxis are relatively inexpensive in Nairobi and other towns, buses and *matatu*s (a kind of minibus) are extremely cheap and an attractive alternative to those on a budget.

However, be aware that every bus and *matatu* in East Africa is loaded with pickpockets who can perform their job easily because the vehicles are so wildly crowded that you're literally squeezed from every side. Make sure when you travel by bus or *matatu* that all your valuables are buried deep within tight-fitting clothing. Backpacks and hand luggage are especially risky propositions unless they are in your lap with your arms around them. I've even had hands reach up inside my well-tucked-in T-shirt for my money belt. The bottom line? Take a taxi.

Bogus Currency

Do not exchange U.S. or European currencies for shillings on the street in either Tanzania or Kenya. Counterfeit bills are everywhere. You'll be especially hassled to exchange your money on the street in Nairobi, Namanga (a border town on the way to Moshi, between Nairobi and Arusha), and Dar es Salaam.

Exchange your cash at either a Forex Bureau or a bank. Barclays, the huge English bank, has offices throughout Kenya.

Sponsorship Requests

No matter where you go in East Africa, you'll be asked to sponsor something. Often, it's school children requesting sponsorship for school supplies. The child will usually have a school notebook with a list of sponsors scrawled on the first page. Much of the time, the list is bogus, and any money you might give the child goes into his pocket for everything but school supplies.

Double Standard Prices

Most of you who buy this guidebook are *mzungu*s (Swahili for "white person"). To many East Africans, *mzungu* means money, so you'll often be charged more than the local people for products and services—sometimes triple. If you don't mind such overbilling, fine. I don't like it, so whenever I'm on Kilimanjaro or Mount Kenya, I try to get a guide or a porter to purchase goods and services for me.

Likewise, many shops don't have prices on items. When you walk through the door, the prices go up. Try to shop where the prices are marked.

Overbilling

During one trip up Mount Kenya, a friend and I bought $250 worth of food at a small supermarket in a town near the base of the mountain. We piled all our chosen items onto the counter, and the store manager began totaling the purchases on a calculator. He didn't know I was keeping track and casually rang up fifteen candy bars when there were ten, two boxes of biscuits when there was one, and so on. He also piled items in such a way that he rang several things up twice. Keep track of your purchases if you want a sane price.

Sirimon Gate, Mount Kenya (Photo © Cameron M. Burns)

Illegitimate Tour Operators

Since a special license is not required for guiding or portering on Mount Kenya, the following rip-off applies only to Kilimanjaro.

Tour operators—even tour operators running mountain trips—must have a government license to operate within Kilimanjaro National Park. However, there are many companies out there who don't have licenses and who will try to sell you a climb. Ask to see their license.

Many legitimate companies hang photocopies of their licenses on the office wall so the originals don't get too ratty. If you are concerned, ask to see the original document. Some unscrupulous firms will obtain a legitimate company's license, photocopy the document, white-out the other company's name, write in their own, then photocopy the document again so it looks the same as the legitimate firm's license hanging on the wall. Although climbing Kilimanjaro with an unlicensed firm will likely be no problem as far as park officials are concerned, some of these illegitimate companies are notorious for bad service.

Paying Park Fees

Because you are required to hire an outfitter to climb Kilimanjaro, the Kilimanjaro National Park fees will be handled for you by the tour company as part of the overall price of the climb. However, with Mount Kenya, you should pay the park fees yourself, personally. Mount Kenya National Park wardens are extremely meticulous with the paperwork of trekkers and mountaineers. Don't entrust paying the park fees to your outfitter—who may or may not be honest.

During a trip up the Burguret Route on Mount Kenya, my climbing partner and I hired a well-known tour operator in Chogoria to organize seven porters and a cook for us and to pay our park entrance fees. While my partner and I, the cook, and all the porters traveled to Nanyuki and began hiking up the mountain, the operator was supposed to travel around to the park's Naro Moru headquarters and pay the entrance and camping fees for two climbers for 18 days, our cook for 18 days, and the porters for 10 days.

After coming down from the mountain, I went over the fee system with park warden Bongo Woodley and discovered that this operator had written into the park records only that two nonresidents of Kenya would be on the mountain for 3 days and had paid the park only Ksh 6,352 (about US$117). He had not paid any of the porters and cook's entrance fees and had pocketed the rest of the Ksh 30,328 (about US$561) we had given him for the park fees. My climbing partner and

I had therefore spent 15 days, and the porters and cook all of their time, in the park illegally. The warden could easily have had us arrested but fortunately decided that a better option would be to bill the tour operator for the rest of the money owed.

Booking Your Own Climb

If, before you leave the United States or Europe, you want to make a reservation for your climb on specific dates, shop around. You can pay anywhere from US$500 to several thousand dollars for an ascent of Kilimanjaro, depending on how you go about it.

If you contact a travel agent in the United States, for example, and ask to book a climb, you will likely be charged two to three times the amount you would pay if you booked your climb in Moshi. This is because your local travel agent will need to call an adventure travel company that specializes in mountain climbing. Often the adventure travel company is also based in North America, so it will need to call another company in Nairobi to book your climb. The Nairobi company, in turn, calls a tour operator in Moshi and books your climb.

Although the Moshi company that actually does all the work might only charge the Nairobi company US$500 for your climb, the Nairobi company will turn around and charge the adventure travel company $700. The adventure travel company will likewise turn around and charge your local travel agent $1,000 for your climb. Your local travel agent might then turn around and charge you $1,200.

VISAS

A visa is nothing more than a stamp that representatives of a country place in your passport before you go to that country. Depending on where you get your visa, prices, requirements, and the time required to get the stamp can vary.

Probably the simplest way to get a visa is to call the embassy of the particular country in your homeland and ask them to send you a tourist visa application. You'll get a several-page questionnaire that must be completed, then submitted to the embassy along with two photographs of yourself, the fee for the visa, and your passport. You must also include a photocopy of your return tickets, showing that you'll be leaving the country. Without proof of your planned departure, your visa application will not be completed. Some officials might even require a letter from your travel agent stating that you will be leaving the country on a particular date via a specific booking.

I recommend sending all this material to the Kenyan or Tanzanian embassies via Federal Express. Make sure you include a prepaid return FedEx envelope and airbill.

You can request either single-entry or multiple-entry visas. A single-entry visa costs about US$30 if bought in the United States and works fine if you're planning to go solely to Tanzania or Kenya. However, if you plan to go in and out of either country (say, land in Nairobi, then travel by land to Kilimanjaro, then return to Nairobi before flying home), you'll need the multiple-entry visa, which costs about US$45 if bought in the United States.

You can also get your visa when you arrive in Kenya or Tanzania (generally cheaper), but be prepared to wait, and have your photos, return ticket, and some cash for your visa fee ready.

Addresses for Tanzanian and Kenya embassies abroad are listed in Appendix A.

HEALTH PRECAUTIONS

Fortunately, the ailments you're likely to encounter in East Africa are easily treated and rarely life-threatening. The most common ailment is simply an upset stomach, and most of the time this is the result of your body adapting to the bacteria of East African cuisine and water.

If you do feel ill, talk to your outfitter. Outfitters are used to dealing with all sorts of ailments and are familiar with problems that visiting Westerners are most likely to experience, and they know where the best and fastest medical help is. You don't have to cut your trip short if you get a bug—if you have it diagnosed early.

African medical facilities have a terrible reputation because of the prevalence of AIDS and other serious diseases. However, for the more common ailments you're likely to encounter, diagnosis and treatment can be accomplished without ever drawing blood or cutting into the body.

Immunizations

There are several immunizations that you should get before leaving North America or Europe for East Africa. At the bare minimum, they should include vaccinations for yellow fever, cholera, hepatitis A, tetanus, polio, typhoid, and meningococcal meningitis. Although medical professionals the world over agree that cholera shots are generally unnecessary, many governments—including those of East Africa—require the cholera stamp on your health documents. (Health documents are simply records of the immunizations you have received. Every public or private medical facility that administers immunizations provides you with these documents at no extra cost.)

Also, if you are planning to get the above-mentioned shots, plan early. Some of them require several courses spread over weeks, even months, and some cannot be taken with other injections.

Malaria

Malaria tablets are also necessary in East Africa. There are several brands available (you can buy them at chemist's shops and many hotels, restaurants, and bars), and some even sell for pennies per tablet. However, according to some medical professionals, some brands of malaria medicine are not effective.

Larium is reportedly the best antimalarial; however, it is not readily available in East Africa. It is also remarkably expensive, costing around US$150 to $200 for the typical course.

Dysentery

Perhaps the most common ailment besides diarrhea is dysentery. There are several kinds, but they all can be identified by severe stomach cramps and confirmed by a simple stool test, which can be done at any "dispensary" (pharmacy).

Water

Although water can be bad in East Africa, it's generally safe to drink in places like Nairobi, Arusha, Moshi, and the villages around Mount Kenya. If you ask whether the water has been chlorinated, as some guidebooks suggest, you will either get an emphatic yes, regardless of whether it has been chlorinated or not, or no answer at all, as many local people are not sure what chlorination is. Most travelers, including climbers, rely on bottled mineral water, which is readily available.

On Mount Kenya and Kilimanjaro, the water is extremely clean, except for those few places where it has been contaminated by human waste. However, unless you are very high on either mountain and the water is draining directly out of a glacier, it is a good idea to boil your water at all times.

Water is readily available at most camps and huts. At worst, such as Barafu Huts on Kilimanjaro, it's a couple of hours' easy hiking away.

Stream below the Machame Huts, Machame Route, Kilimanjaro
(Photo © Cameron M. Burns)

ACCIDENTS AND GETTING LOST

Both Kilimanjaro and Mount Kenya National Parks are set up to respond to emergencies. Both have rescue teams, although their knowledge and experience is considerably less than one would expect of the European or North American equivalent.

If you are in an accident in which a member of your group is injured and cannot be moved, you should contact park rescue personnel as quickly as possible.

On Kilimanjaro, rescue personnel are stationed at all the huts along the Marangu Route. You can also contact park personnel at any of the main gates: Marangu, Mweka, Umbwe, Machame, Shira, and Rongai.

On Mount Kenya, rescue personnel are permanently stationed at the ranger station at the head of the Teleki Valley, on the Naro Moru Route, just up from Mackinder's Camp. You can also contact park personnel at any of the main gates: Chogoria, Sirimon, and Naro Moru.

If there are more than two in your party, one member should stay with the injured person while the other goes for help. If there are only two of you, the uninjured member should provide the victim with easy access to food, water, and clothing before going for help. If you are leaving an injured climber on a technical mountaineering route, make sure the person is well anchored to the rock.

Before leaving an injured climber, write down all information on the victim's condition and location, and mark the location on a map.

If you can lend a hand in a rescue, by all means do so. It may be hours before official park personnel arrive on the scene, and by that time you and a few other volunteers could easily have carried a mountain sickness victim to a lower elevation and saved the person's life. Altitude sicknesses, which are by far the greatest

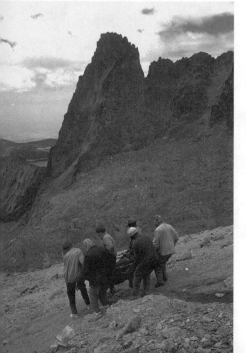

Evacuating a mountain sickness victim from the Austrian Hut, with Point John in the background, Mount Kenya
(Photo © Cameron M. Burns)

threat to anyone on Kilimanjaro and Mount Kenya, can kill someone in just a few hours.

If you get lost, stay where you are. Wandering around trying to regain a trail can get you more lost. Lay a brightly colored article of clothing near yourself so that searchers on the ground and in the air can see it. Try to find an open place, and do not wander into thick forest or jungle. It is typical that lost climbers will be out overnight.

In all cases, you will be expected to pay for your rescue. Fortunately, rescue costs in East Africa are much cheaper than in North America or Europe. (See Fees, under Kilimanjaro and Mount Kenya Regulations and Fees sections of Chapter 3.)

WILDLIFE

During one of his attempts on Kibo from the northeast, first ascensionist Hans Meyer discovered the body of a small antelope very near the summit. A leopard was also found near the summit in 1926 by Dr. Reusch. The remains of a Sykes monkey can be found on the second pitch of the Normal Route on Mount Kenya, reportedly lured there with food by British soldiers. And a black serval was seen several years ago near Austrian Hut by a friend of mine.

Despite these stories, animals are rarely found high on either Kilimanjaro or Mount Kenya. It is in the forest and moorland areas that climbers need to be aware of East Africa's unpredictable wildlife.

On both mountains—but especially on Mount Kenya—the biggest danger is the Cape buffalo *(Syncerus caffer),* sometimes called the African Buffalo. Buffalo are monstrous creatures that can weigh up to 800 kilograms (1,764 pounds). They are herd animals that prefer open grassland areas and generally congregate around watering places. For the most part, buffalo are docile animals that will wander off when you approach. However, if they are surprised, or have young, they can charge. The best thing to do is make a lot of noise when wandering through forested areas and to keep your distance when you do see one.

As with buffalo, elephants *(Loxodonta africana)* are known to charge if surprised or with young. Again, make a lot of noise and keep your distance.

Baboons and monkeys can be found throughout the forests on Kilimanjaro and Mount Kenya. They pose no physical threat, but they love to steal sunglasses, cameras, articles of clothing, and small backpacks.

Rock hyraxes *(Procavia capensis)* are strange little mammals, similar in size, shape, and color to American and European marmots. Oddly,

Chameleon on the Marangu Route, near the Mandara Hut, Kilimanjaro
(Photo © Cameron M. Burns)

they are the closest living relative to the elephant. They are extremely common on Mount Kenya, but rare on Kilimanjaro, where rumor has it that porters have eaten them all. Like marmots, hyraxes will rummage through campsites looking for anything to eat. They have been known to chew into backpacks and bags left unattended. Stow your belongings carefully if you are planning to leave them for any length of time.

Big cats (lions, leopards) are rare on both Kilimanjaro and Mount Kenya and should be of no concern, as they generally keep out of the way of humans and tend not to go very high on the mountains.

Servals *(Felis serval)*, long-legged wild cats about the size of a domestic cat, are common on both mountains but are shy and retiring nocturnal creatures.

Other animals you can expect to see on Kilimanjaro include the dik-dik, bushbuck, duiker, wart hog, chameleon, mongoose, and sunbird. Occasionally, a zebra or hyena will wander up onto the Shira Plateau.

On Mount Kenya, which has vastly more wildlife than Kilimanjaro, you might encounter all the creatures mentioned above, along with eland and waterbuck. Black rhinoceros *(Diceros bicornis)* have occasionally been reported on Mount Kenya; if you see one, you should consider yourself very lucky.

CHAPTER 3

CLIMBING IN EAST AFRICA

PLANNING THE TRIP

The amount of time needed to climb Kilimanjaro or Mount Kenya is much shorter than the amount of time needed to climb other high mountains of the world. I know of climbers who have done Mount Kenya's Chogoria–Naro Moru traverse with a quick run up to Point Lenana in 3 days. On the other hand, a German naturalist recently took 12 days for an ascent of Kilimanjaro, spending dozens of hours observing the flora and fauna and taking notes and photographs as he gradually ascended the mountain.

There are no absolutes, but most parties take 5 or 6 days to ascend any of the standard trekking routes on either Kilimanjaro or Mount Kenya. If a technical mountaineering route is to be part of the ascent as well, add another 2 to 3 days.

Besides the time needed on the mountain, it generally takes a day to reach either Kilimanjaro or Mount Kenya by road from Nairobi and another day to get back to Nairobi; a couple of days' rest here and there along the way is highly recommended.

Most climbers going to Kili spend a night in Nairobi, then take the Davanu shuttle to Moshi the following morning. It is also beneficial to then spend at least one day in Moshi, Arusha, or Marangu doing nothing but sleeping and resting before beginning an ascent. The long flight from North America or Europe wears you down, and your body needs at least a full day to adjust to the local food.

Because you're traveling halfway around the globe, you may want to add an extra week onto your trip for a safari, the consummate East African experience.

Seasons and Weather

There are two climbing seasons in East Africa: mid-December through mid-March, and early June through mid-October. Both of these periods are considered "dry seasons" in East Africa. Mid-December through mid-March is dry and warm, whereas early June through mid-October is generally dry and cool. The highest tourist season on both Kilimanjaro and Mount Kenya is probably the warm dry season, especially around Christmas.

Despite these broad generalizations, there are always regional and local fluctuations in the weather. Kilimanjaro and Mount Kenya are so tall and isolated from other ranges that they create their own weather. After a clear morning, thick cloud cover forms around their summits (4,000 meters and up) around 10:00 A.M., remaining until late in the day, when the summits clear for the night.

During the dry seasons, precipitation is infrequent, but not unheard of. Compared with mountains of a similar height in other parts of the world, Kilimanjaro and Mount Kenya seem to have fewer windy periods. However, when the wind does blow, it can be extremely fierce.

Most routes on Kilimanjaro and Mount Kenya can be climbed in either dry season. Routes on Mount Kenya are more weather-dependent. Rock routes that face south are best done in December, January, and February; routes that face north are best in July, August, and September. Ice climbs are just the opposite: south-facing routes are best done in July, August, and September; north-facing routes are best in December, January, and February.

Although both mountains sit astride the equator, both Kilimanjaro and Mount Kenya can be extremely cold places, especially during the night. Generally, expect temperatures at night and in the early morning at the 4,600-meter level to be as low as minus 5 degrees Celsius (23 degrees Fahrenheit).

Daytime temperatures are much more reasonable. It is possible to wear shorts as far as the top huts (Kibo, Barafu, Arrow Glacier, Austrian, Kami, and so forth) on both mountains, where midday temperatures can reach 10 degrees Celsius (50 degrees Fahrenheit).

However, anyone climbing above the 4,600-meter level should have several thermal layers of clothing. Also, be prepared to feel cooler at noon than you do at 9:00 A.M. or 4:00 P.M. The moisture in the clouds that swirl around the summits during the day makes the air feel much colder than it really is.

Choosing a Climbing Partner

Visitors to Kilimanjaro National Park (commonly called KINAPA) are required to travel with a registered guide anytime they go inside the park boundaries, even if it's for a short day hike, and even if there is more than one person in the group. Because of this requirement, a climbing partner is unnecessary on Kili, and many choose to climb the mountain with only their required guide. (For more on climbing regulations in KINAPA, see Kilimanjaro Regulations and Fees, below.)

Because most of the guides and porters on Kili have limited English, if you choose to climb the mountain without a partner, you'll spend a lot of time hanging out by yourself while the guide has a good time with his porter friends. In short, it's a lonely experience. I recommend going with at least one other person on any Kili route, even the trekking routes.

Land Rovers passing en route to the Rongai Route trailhead, Kilimanjaro (Photo © Cameron M. Burns)

For the technical mountaineering routes on Kilimanjaro, knowledge of ice and alpine climbing techniques is essential. Unlike Mount Kenya, there are no technical routes on Kili that are purely rock climbs.

On Mount Kenya, park regulations don't require climbers to have guides or porters. You and your partner can go climb by yourselves, wherever you like. Some tour operators might try to convince you that you must have a guide or porters on Mount Kenya, which is untrue. However, because of safety concerns, park regulations prohibit anyone from entering the park alone. (For more on climbing regulations in Mount Kenya National Park, see Mount Kenya Regulations and Fees, below.)

As with Kilimanjaro, for both trekking and technical mountaineering on Mount Kenya, I thoroughly recommend going with at least one partner, even if you just met the person in Nairobi.

For the trekking routes on Kibo (Normal, Barafu, and Western Breach Routes) and Mount Kenya (Point Lenana), experience with high altitude is not essential, but it can certainly help. Experience with long, hard day hikes, especially those that go above 3,000 meters, can be extremely useful.

For the technical mountaineering routes on both Kili and Mount Kenya, basic rock and ice climbing skills are necessary, but high-altitude mountaineering experience is not a prerequisite.

OUTFITTERS
Kilimanjaro
One thing you'll notice when you arrive in Tanzania is that there are probably a couple of hundred companies offering guided treks up Kilimanjaro. Only Tanzanian-owned businesses are allowed to operate within Tanzanian national parks.

I asked Matthew Mombo, Kilimanjaro National Park warden, which tour operators working on Kilimanjaro were the best, and he recommended the handful of outfitters listed in Appendix A. If you are interested in looking into other firms, I suggest picking up a copy of one of the Lonely Planet guides to East Africa (see Appendix C: Further Reading). However, remember that the companies listed in those guides constitute about one-thirtieth of the companies that offer Kili climbs.

Also, if you have any questions about tour operators, the park warden is available to discuss firms with you. You can write to him, but mail takes weeks, even months to get to Tanzania and back to the United States or Europe. And, to tell the truth, I've never, ever received a written response from KINAPA officials by mail. The best thing to do is go to the park office at the Marangu gate and try to catch the warden or one of his assistants there. Be prepared to wait around for a couple of hours.

The costs of climbing Kilimanjaro with an outfitter vary wildly, depending on where and how you book your climb (see Avoiding Rip-offs in Chapter 2). Most outfitter-arranged climbs booked in Moshi, Arusha, or Marangu currently range between US$500 and $700 per person. Although this may sound expensive, it is important to factor in how much of these costs are going to park fees (see Kilimanjaro Regulations and Fees, below). Of US$500 for a 5-day ascent of the Marangu Route, for example, you'll quickly see that about $350 to $370 is going into park fees. Since outfitters generally include the costs of trailhead transportation in the overall price of a climb and renting vehicles is phenomenally expensive, these prices should begin to seem like a bargain. Besides trailhead transportation and national park fees, the prices an outfitter quotes should include food, cooking equipment, and a tent, if one is needed.

There are also some differences in price between the Marangu Route and other routes, which are more difficult to access. Marangu is the cheapest, and likely always will be. The Machame–Mweka combination route is probably next cheapest (around US$600 to $700). The Shira Plateau and Rongai Routes are the most expensive (US$700 and up) because they require a half day's travel to reach the trailheads.

All prices are generally negotiable.

Mount Kenya

As for Kilimanjaro, I asked Mount Kenya National Park officials to recommend reputable tour operators who offer guide, porter, transportation, and other services. The list appears in Appendix A.

A few years ago, dozens of tour operators, hoteliers, and porter/guide associations organized themselves into the Association of Mount Kenya Operators (AMKO) to promote tourism and improve the standards of tourist operators on and around Mount Kenya. All the outfitters listed in Appendix A are AMKO members.

You can also always get an outfitter recommendation from park officials. The park warden's office is located at the park gate on the Naro Moru Route.

There are some key differences between outfitters on Kili and Mount Kenya. For one thing, most outfitters on Mount Kenya only take clients or groups up Point Lenana, the third-highest summit on the massif.

The standard 4-day trips up to Lenana run anywhere between US$300 and $500, depending on the company (see Avoiding Rip-offs in Chapter 2).

One British friend recently did a 4-day trip up Point Lenana for US$80. He saved money by taking *matatus* from Nairobi, then walked the entire 30 kilometers from Chogoria to the Chogoria Gate; on his way out, he walked from the Sirimon Gate down to Nanyuki. His only expenses were park fees and the stingy US$5 per day he spent on his porter/guide.

Ascents to the summits of Nelion and Batian are requested infrequently and are considered a specialty product. Guides will ask a wide variety of sums for the ascent (anywhere from US$100 to $300 for the summit alone). The more expensive guides are white and/or Nairobi based. Many locals living in the villages around Mount Kenya guide Nelion and Batian for very modest fees and make better company on the mountain than the Nairobi-based hotshots. However, they often lack basic gear.

Should you plan to put together your own trip up to Lenana or Batian/Nelion, which I recommend, you will likely pay between US$8 and $9 a day for porters, and a few extra dollars per day for a seasoned guide (negotiable).

Outfitters who arrange porters and guides for you will add on a booking fee, as will most hotels who arrange porters and guides, which can double the daily cost of a porter or guide. The eastern side of the mountain is much less expensive for hiring porters and guides than the tourist-oriented western side with its expensive lodges and package tours.

EQUIPMENT

For both trekking and technical mountaineering on Kilimanjaro and Mount Kenya, remarkably little gear is needed compared with climbing similar-sized mountains in other parts of the world.

However, Kilimanjaro is nearly 6,000 meters, and Mount Kenya is over 5,000 meters, and both can be extremely cold at times. Extremely cold!

Following are my recommendations of necessary equipment, divided into two lists: one for trekkers or nontechnical climbers and a second

Typical footwear worn by porters on Kilimanjaro
(Photo © Cameron M. Burns)

specifically for technical mountaineers. The latter will obviously want to bring most of the items listed in the trekkers' list.

On Kilimanjaro, the most important gear consideration comes after you've booked your climb with an outfitter: the tent. For all routes other than the Marangu Route, it is advisable to bring a tent.

There are huts on many of the routes, but these are in such a bad state of repair that few climbers use them. Porters and guides use the huts for cooking, so they have soot-coated walls and piles of firewood in them. Most outfitters can provide tents for Kili, but I recommend bringing your own. East African tents are extremely heavy canvas jobs, and because a porter will likely carry it, he'll then have to give more stuff to you to carry. Lightweight tents from North America and Europe are the way to go.

On Mount Kenya, it is also advisable to bring a tent, as you will be more assured of privacy and avoid being hassled by local people illegally trying to extract hut fees from you (see Hut Reservations, below).

Discuss with your outfitter other things you'll need to bring. Most likely you will not need to bring along your own cooking utensils or food, as they will be provided. However, you still might want to bring some of your own food in case the East African mountain food is not palatable.

Also, you must bring a sleeping bag. No outfitters provide them. A bag rated to minus 23 degrees Celsius (minus 10 degrees Fahrenheit) will be adequate.

On both mountains, the best clothing is a collection of items that can be layered one over the other as you ascend to colder areas. Fleece and polypropylene items work well, and you should plan on bringing at least three layers, not counting a shell system to go over the thermal layers. Cotton clothing is not a good idea at the higher and colder elevations. Although this warning will sound ridiculous to experienced mountaineers, I've seen dozens of climbers on both Kilimanjaro and Mount Kenya wearing cotton socks and cotton turtle-necked shirts.

Bring everything you need from home, as there are no climbing or outdoor equipment shops in East Africa, and the few rental shops that have gear offer junk.

TREKKERS / NONTECHNICAL CLIMBERS

Footwear
Sturdy trekking boots or walking shoes (plastic mountaineering boots are unnecessary)
Heavy-duty socks (3–4 pairs, wool or polypropylene)
Gaiters (to keep out gravel and snow)

Clothing
Shell jacket
Shell pants
Long top and bottom underwear (expedition-weight polypropylene)
Two thermal layers (fleece shirt and pullover)
Long nylon or acrylic walking pants
T-shirt
Shorts
Warm hat
Gloves/mittens

Accessories
Sunglasses
Trekking poles (optional)
Headlamp or flashlight
Spare bulbs
Batteries

Camping / Sleeping Gear
Backpack

Tent
Sleeping bag
Sleeping pad
Stove
Fuel containers
Cooking pots
Cooking kit
Matches/lighter in waterproof container
Firestarter
Water bottles
Water pump

Personal Hygiene

Toothbrush
Toothpaste
Dental floss
Shaving kit
Soap
Toilet paper
Small backpacking towels
Sunblock (very important)
Lip cream with sunblock

Miscellaneous

Map
Compass
Whistle
Pocketknife
First-aid kit
Insect repellent
Camera
Film
Journals/pens
Zippered plastic bags
Sewing kit
Extra food
Extra clothing

TECHNICAL MOUNTAINEERS

Mountaineering boots (leather boots work fine)
Helmet
Harness

Crampons (flexible, twelve-point crampons work fine)
Ice tools/axes
Extra ice picks and accessories
Carabiners (30)
Slings or runners (10)
Ropes, 50 meters x 8 millimeters (2)
Set of wired stoppers (usually 8–10)
Ice screws (6–10)
Full set of camming units with half sizes
Goggles
Technical daypack
Bivy sack

TREKKING VERSUS TECHNICAL MOUNTAINEERING

The biggest problem with putting together a book like this is differentiating between technical mountaineering (with ropes, hardware, and so forth) and trekking (without equipment), which is also called walking or hiking.

Also, there is scrambling, which is hiking on very steep ground, with use of the hands needed for balance and upward progress. Trekkers often consider scrambling at the upper end of their abilities; technical mountaineers consider it at the lower end.

Where I grew up, "climbers" were technical mountaineering types who used ropes, hardware, and special skills for an ascent. However, most people who reach the summit of Kilimanjaro consider themselves climbers. For this book, I have decided to lump everyone together as climbers, whether they are doing a walking route or a serious Grade VI technical climb.

To differentiate between the two groups, I refer to the ropes-and-hardware group as "technical mountaineers."

"Trekkers" are therefore those who do not use ropes and hardware for climbing, and "trekking routes" are routes that require no technical mountaineering skills or equipment.

In this guidebook, I have described six major forest and moorland routes on Kilimanjaro (Marangu, Mweka, Umbwe, Machame, Shira Plateau, and Rongai) and five forest and moorland routes on Mount Kenya (Naro Moru, Sirimon, Burguret, Timau, and Chogoria). These routes lead through the forests to the base of the main peaks on both mountains. All can be walked by trekkers (and must be walked by technical mountaineers if they want to get to the main peaks to climb!).

The summits are a different matter. On Kilimanjaro, there are two trekking routes to the summit of Kibo, Kili's highest peak: the Normal Route and the Barafu Route. A third route up Kibo, the Western Breach Route, is often called a trekking route, but it involves scrambling and is therefore not pure trekking.

There are no trekking routes to the two highest summits of Mount Kenya: Batian and Nelion. However, there are trekking routes on Mount Kenya's third-highest summit, Point Lenana.

Distinctions as to whether a route requires technical mountaineering skills and equipment—or, conversely, can be done in just hiking boots—will become obvious in individual route descriptions.

CLIMBING GRADES

This guidebook uses the East African grading system for climbs. For technical mountaineering routes (hard climbs), the system uses numbers between Grade I and Grade VII. For routes that fall into the category of "trekking" (walks and hikes), the East African system uses three simple descriptive phrases to grade climbs: "walk," "stiff walk," and "scramble."

Although American and European rock climbers might not appreciate the East African grading system at first, as it is vague in terms of individual moves, it actually makes a lot of sense in mountaineering situations. As any mountaineer knows, it's often possible to avoid one variation of a route and climb another, and conditions—and therefore grades—change. The East African system also takes into account objective dangers such as rockfall.

Perhaps the most unusual thing about East African grades is that both rock and ice routes are graded under the same system. In other parts of the world, rock ratings and ice ratings are separated. Although the East African system works well in a mountaineering sense, it is sometimes difficult to translate one mountaineer's understanding of a Grade III rock route into a Grade III ice climb. I have therefore added my own comparison of East African grades with American ice climbing grades, using the "water ice" (WI) prefix in the accompanying chart.

Aid ratings (A1 to A6) are based on American aid ratings, as these are now the most commonly used aid ratings in the world.

EAST AFRICAN CLIMBING GRADES

EAST AFRICAN	AMERICAN	AMERICAN WATER ICE	ENGLISH	FRENCH
Walk	Class 1		Walk	
Stiff walk	Class 2		Stiff walk	
Scramble	Class 3		Scramble	
Grade I	Class 4/5.1–5.2		Easy–moderate	F (Facile)
Grade II	Class 5.3	WI 1	Moderate–difficult	PD (Peu Difficile)
Grade III	Class 5.3–5.4	WI 2	Difficult–very difficult	AD (Assez Difficile)
Grade IV	Class 5.5	WI 3	Very difficult–mild severe	D (Difficile)
Grade V	Class 5.6–5.7	WI 4	Severe–very severe	TD (Très Difficile)
Grade VI	Class 5.8	WI 5	Very severe–hard very severe	ED (Extrêmement Difficile)
Grade VII	Class 5.9–5.11	WI 6	Extreme	ABO (Abominable)

None of the routes on Kilimanjaro and Mount Kenya should be considered in terms of their grade alone. These are high mountains, and the weather, the season, your fitness, and your experience with climbing at altitude for extended periods all come into play.

MAPS

Numerous maps of Kilimanjaro and Mount Kenya are available in East Africa, North America, and Europe. Many are poorly made and inaccurate. For Mount Kenya, Andrew Wielochowski and Mark Savage's *Mt Kenya Map and Guide* is generally regarded as the best. This publication, which has been updated over the years, is actually three maps (one of which is a full-sized topographic map) and a condensed technical mountaineering guide all in one. A few years ago, Wielochowski created a similar product for Kilimanjaro, the *Kilimanjaro Map and Guide,* which also includes a full-sized topographic map. One way to get a copy of either of these two excellent maps is to go to any good bookstore in Nairobi. They can also be obtained through specialty shops in Europe and North America that stock maps and climbing guides. (For information on obtaining these and other related maps and guides in England or the United States, see Appendix A.)

The maps included in this guidebook cover the major forest and moorland approach routes on Kilimanjaro and Mount Kenya, as well as the locations of the three trekking summit routes on Kibo and the Nelion/Batian Normal Route on Mount Kenya. In general, the maps do not include the summit routes on Kilimanjaro and Mount Kenya, since placing them on a map does very little to help the reader figure out where they go. Rather, these routes are best described in photographs and literal descriptions, which are included for nearly every summit route on both mountains.

Though a road map can be helpful for general travel in East Africa, do not purchase one specifically for your trip to Kilimanjaro or Mount Kenya. Unfortunately, there are no road maps in existence that accurately and completely depict the intricate network of minor dirt roads that traverse the agricultural lower slopes of these two mountains. In fact, most road maps available for East Africa depict only the major highways (usually the paved ones). In the case of both Kilimanjaro and Mount Kenya, you are unlikely to be driving your own automobile to the trailheads anyway (see Getting to the Mountains, below). Although I have included directions for reaching the trailheads for all the major trails, you may need to stop and ask for directions from locals once you are on the mountains, as roads wash out, bridges collapse, and things, in general, change.

FOOD

Food prepared on the mountains of East Africa by the porters and guides is like the food in the cities, towns, and villages: good, but it takes some getting used to.

It's amazing to watch the local porters and guides lug huge, heavy pots, cans, and bottles up Kili and Mount Kenya, then prepare meals over primitive wood fires. Often, the food is set out on a picnic blanket, and it is always served with tea, a throwback to the colonial days.

Unless you specify otherwise, your guide and porters, who take on the role of cook at mealtime, will likely prepare breakfasts of eggs, sausages, toast, pancakes, and fruit. Lunches are pretty similar, with a chicken wing or lump of cheese thrown in for good measure, and a carrot replacing the fruit. Dinners are generally some kind of meat with rice, potatoes, or *ugali* (a type of cornmeal).

With most outfitters, you can request to bring your own food, or a special kind of diet. I cannot vouch for how good the food will be if that's the case. I've always found it better and easier to eat what they give you. The servings are huge, and it's all cooked to death, so there is little threat of contamination.

If you do decide to bring your own special food on the mountain, bring it from home. There is no such thing as freeze-dried food or anything like it in East Africa.

PHYSICAL FITNESS

Some guidebooks will recommend running, hiking, and other activities before you head off to climb Kilimanjaro or Mount Kenya. While this certainly can't hurt, especially if you live at sea level, I'm not sure how helpful it is.

I have never trained for any climbing on either of these mountains. I find simply taking my time while I'm walking through the forests into the mountains to be more helpful than any aerobic conditioning plan I might follow before leaving home. In fact, if you're not sure how well you'll do at altitude, plan a climb in which you spend a couple of extra nights at the high huts.

If you absolutely must undertake a training regimen, try running or walking 10 to 15 miles per week for 6 to 8 weeks before your departure.

HIGH-ALTITUDE PROBLEMS

The most frequent illnesses mountaineers going to Kilimanjaro and Mount Kenya will encounter are various altitude-related conditions. They are all a result of climbing too high, too fast. And the one common treatment that works best for all three is descent.

There are no hard and fast rules about who will be affected by these illnesses. Some Himalayan experts who have been climbing for years can experience altitude sickness; meanwhile, inexperienced climbers going high for the first time might feel fine all the way to the top of Kilimanjaro.

The major illnesses are outlined below.

Acute Mountain Sickness (AMS)

The most common altitude-related problem is acute mountain sickness (AMS). Like other altitude illnesses, AMS is caused by ascending to high elevations too quickly for the body to adjust. AMS can occur at any altitude but is most likely in the first 1,000 meters of elevation gain during a climb. Generally, its symptoms begin to occur at 2,500 meters (8,000 feet). Those who live at low elevations, fly to East Africa, and get straight on a mountain are especially vulnerable.

Symptoms of AMS include headache, breathlessness, nausea, vomiting, dizziness, a rasping cough, insomnia, and a loss of appetite. To quote Charles Houston, a leading researcher on altitude-related sicknesses, "AMS is much like a bad hangover, and like a hangover usually subsides in a day or two."

One of the worst aspects of AMS is Cheyne-Stokes breathing, also called periodic breathing, which causes a dozing-off victim to suddenly awake gasping for air. This ailment occurs regularly above 2,700 meters (9,000 feet) and can be extremely frustrating.

AMS is easily cured by descending to a lower altitude and resting for a day or two. Generally, after this period of rest, a climb can be resumed.

It is also important to remember that not everything that feels like AMS is AMS. There are many other bugs in East Africa, including the simple flu, that can cause similar symptoms.

High-Altitude Pulmonary Edema (HAPE)

High-altitude pulmonary edema (HAPE), an accumulation of fluid in the lungs, can come on quickly and kill a victim within a few hours. Symptoms include exhaustion, difficulty in breathing, chest pain, a gurgling noise in the chest, and a cough with bloody sputum (saliva mixed with mucus).

The best treatment is to get the victim to a lower elevation as soon as possible, even if that means carrying the person. Oxygen is often used to treat HAPE on mountaineering expeditions, but the best treatment is a fast and immediate descent.

High-Altitude Cerebral Edema (HACE)

High-altitude cerebral edema (HACE) is the most serious altitude-related illness and is caused by a lack of oxygen. The large and small arteries of the brain dilate so they can carry more blood and more oxygen, causing the brain to swell.

One of the obvious results of this swelling, or cerebral edema, is a tremendous headache. Other symptoms are confusion, hallucination, an inability to control emotions, and a staggering walk.

As with HAPE, it is essential to get the victim to a lower elevation as quickly as possible. Carry the person if you must!

Acclimatization

There are a few simple rules that you should swear by if you plan to reach the summits of any peaks in East Africa.

First, climb slowly. The expression *"pole-pole"* ("slowly, slowly" in Swahili) is well known as a climber's mantra in East Africa. A slow ascent will always produce better results than a fast one.

Above 1,500 meters (5,000 feet), experts recommend taking a full day for every 300 meters (1,000 feet) of elevation increase. For most climbers headed to East Africa, this is sometimes difficult because of time considerations. If time and budget allow, plan on spending one or two extra nights on the mountain. The extra time will help you acclimatize and increase your chances of reaching the summit.

"If one member of the party shows signs of HAPE or HACE, slow down, stop, or turn back before the problem escalates," Houston once wrote. "There will be other days, other mountains."

Also, don't let your guide rush you. Guides and porters are notorious for this on the descent. Certainly they're eager to get home, but occasionally they will set a pace on the ascent that is unreasonable.

Set your own pace and don't be pressured into going at a speed you cannot handle.

Second, drink a lot of water. Acclimatization is much easier for a well-hydrated body than a dehydrated body. Drink at least 4 liters per day—6 liters if you can. Avoid diuretics such as coffee and tea, as well as alcohol and drugs.

Many climbers like to use Diamox (acetazolamide), a drug that is often effective in preventing mild altitude sickness. However, the negative side effects of Diamox (massive urination and evacuation) are so powerful for some people that I strongly recommend against its use.

Hypothermia and Frostbite

Kilimanjaro and Mount Kenya lack the extremely cold temperatures found in many mountain ranges of the world, but hypothermia and frostbite can still occur.

Hypothermia is a condition in which the body's core temperature drops below normal. The victim becomes weak and often begins to shake. The obvious response is to warm the victim by providing warm liquids, high-energy foods, hot-water bottles, and even crawling into a sleeping bag with the person (both of you nude for better heat transfer).

In frostbite, soft tissue is destroyed as body fluids freeze into crystals around the cells of the tissue. In the initial stages, the skin is white and hard.

In mild frostbite, when the skin is still soft (sometimes called "frostnip"), the affected area can be rewarmed fairly easily by placing the part someplace warm—under an arm, in a sleeping bag, in the crotch, or against the bare skin of a companion (the chest is good). The rewarming process may be painful, but is usually without long-term problems.

When an appendage is seriously affected by frostbite, the best thing to do is to evacuate the victim without rewarming the frostbitten area. Rewarming a frostbitten area generally causes more damage than the actual frostbite. A victim can walk out on frostbitten feet but must be carried if the feet are rewarmed.

If your evacuation must include another night out, rewarming the frostbitten area is inevitable. Modern medical thinking now dictates that rewarming be done quickly. Use water between 38 and 41 degrees Celsius (100 to 105 degrees Fahrenheit) and soak the frostbitten part for 30 minutes. Do not massage the affected flesh in any way. Once the frostbitten area is warm, wrap it with a loose bandage and keep it warm until a full evacuation can be made. Refreezing of a frostbitten part will cause further damage.

The best prevention for both hypothermia and frostbite is to dress properly. Dress in wools and fleece fabrics; never wear cotton clothing! You should also keep yourself well hydrated and well fed.

GETTING TO THE MOUNTAINS

Once you're in East Africa, getting to Kilimanjaro or Mount Kenya is fairly easy, although the options are not limitless.

The Kilimanjaro area is served by an international airport, Kilimanjaro International Airport (KIA), as well as by various buses and shuttles. The Mount Kenya area is served by tiny airstrips, but many of these are private and arranging a flight to them is almost impossible.

Only the most popular—and most cost-effective—ways of getting to the mountains are outlined here.

To/From Kilimanjaro

From Nairobi or Dar, you can either fly to Kilimanjaro International Airport, 64 kilometers west of Moshi, or travel by bus or train.

KLM, Corsair (Air France), and a number of African airlines—such as South African Airlines, Air Tanzania, and Malawi Air—run regular flights between Nairobi and KIA; the flight, however, is incredibly expensive. For example, KLM currently charges about US$370 round trip from Nairobi to KIA. Remember that you will also have to pay about Tsh 20,000 (US$40) for the taxi ride from KIA to Moshi, as well as airport departure taxes in both Nairobi and Tanzania.

A much cheaper way to get to Moshi from Nairobi—and the only real option to flying—is the Davanu shuttle. Many older guidebooks refer to the DHL shuttle between Nairobi and Moshi; however, this shuttle was discontinued in 1996. The route was taken over by the folks at Davanu, who run an excellent service for about US$40 round trip and about US$35 one way. The best way to save money is to buy a return ticket and keep the return date open.

The Davanu shuttle leaves from a small depot opposite the Norfolk Hotel on Harry Thuku Road in Nairobi every morning at about 8:30 A.M. You can simply show up there and buy a ticket, or you can arrange for the shuttle to pick you up at your hotel as it heads out of town. Make sure you ask your hotel's concierge to call Davanu the night before and request a pickup. There is no limit on luggage. If there's too much, it gets piled on the roof.

The drive south across the plains is pleasant, and relatively safe. Along the way you will see zebra, ostrich, and Thomson's gazelles ("Tommies"). You're also likely to see giraffes, warthogs, and secretary birds.

The shuttle crosses the border at Namanga. If it's your first time in Africa, Namanga will scare you. Imposing Masai men and women thrust beads, carvings, and trinkets of all manner in the shuttle windows at you with persistence. For reference, the same trinkets are much cheaper in the discount shops along Muindi Mbingu Street in Nairobi or in the Nairobi City Market.

You will be required to get off the shuttle and go through Kenyan and Tanzanian customs, but this process is fairly quick—as long as you can duck past the Masai trinket-sellers.

The shuttle then heads for Arusha, where it takes a 1-hour break at the Novotel Hotel, then goes on to Moshi, about 1.5 hours away. In all, it takes about 6 hours to get from Nairobi to Moshi. In Moshi, Davanu has a tiny office opposite the Moshi Hotel, where it drops you off.

For the return journey, the shuttle leaves from the Davanu office in Moshi at about 10:30 A.M.

If you want to travel on to the tiny village of Marangu, it's possible to get a bus for about US$1 at the bus station in downtown Moshi on Mawenzi Road. A taxi from Moshi to Marangu will cost you about Tsh 15,000 to 20,000 (US$30 to $40). Taxis around Moshi and Arusha should run you about Tsh 1,500 to 2,000 (US$3 to $4) for a 5- to 10-minute ride. Always ask the price before you get in.

If you're coming from Dar, buses run daily from the station on the corner of Morogoro Road and Libya Street. There is no central bus station in Dar. There are both "express" buses, as well as regular buses. However, both seem to take about the same amount of time and make as many stops. An express bus will cost you between Tsh 8,000 and 9,000 (about US$16 to $18). A regular bus will cost about half that. The ride takes about 8 to 10 hours.

It is also possible to catch a *matatu* from Nairobi to Namanga, but getting one from Namanga south to Arusha is, apparently, somewhat difficult because you must walk across the border and take a Tanzanian *matatu* for the ride to Arusha. You can catch a *matatu* in the River Road–Accra Road area in Nairobi. Few trekkers and climbers use *matatus* to get to Kilimanjaro, but they are popular for transportation to and from

Mount Kenya. (For a greater explanation of *matatus*, see To/From Mount Kenya, below.)

It's also possible to take a bus from Mombasa direct to Moshi via Taveta, on the border, without going through Nairobi. This costs around Tsh 2,000 (US$4). *Matatus* also travel the Mombasa–Moshi route, but it is often necessary to change *matatus* at Taveta or Voi, on the Nairobi–Mombasa Road.

To/From Mount Kenya

There are many different options for getting to and from Mount Kenya from Nairobi. For one thing, a paved tarmac road leads north out of Nairobi to Sagana Junction, where it intersects with a paved tarmac ring road that circles Mount Kenya and connects all the towns (Naro Moru, Nanyuki, Timau, Meru, Chogoria, Chuka, Embu) scattered around the base of the mountain.

It's about 3.5 to 4 hours' drive from Nairobi to either Naro Moru or Chogoria, plus another 1 to 2 hours from Naro Moru to Nanyuki, on the northwest side of the mountain. (It's about a 3-hour drive from Chogoria to Nanyuki.)

The easiest but most expensive option for getting to any town around the base of the mountain, even from Nairobi, is to hire a taxi. I've done this a couple of times. The first time I did, four German climbers told me not to pay more than Ksh 10,000 (US$200) for the service. I actually ended up getting a cab for Ksh 6,500 (US$130) from Nairobi to Chogoria. On the return trip, a friend was able to hire me a taxi for Ksh 4,000 (US$80).

A much cheaper, but much more dangerous, way of getting to Mount Kenya is to go by *matatu*. *Matatus*—the equivalent of the Latin American *collectivo* taxi—are minibuses designed to carry about ten people, but generally they carry twenty-five or more.

Matatu drivers speed like demons, swerve around corners, force other drivers off the road, and generally wreak havoc. Half the time you're in one, someone is sitting on your lap because there's not enough room. *Matatus* have names like Rambo 2000, Excessive Force, and The Babe Coach. Every single day that you're in East Africa, you can pick up the newspaper and read about deaths from the previous day's *matatu* accidents. I remember one day in which the *matatu* death toll was eighteen!

Regardless, a *matatu* ride from Nairobi to Chogoria or Naro Moru will cost you between Ksh 250 and 400 (US$5 to $8), but if you have a pack or two full of camping or climbing gear, you may be required to pay for the space taken up by your luggage. Once you're in Embu, Chuka, Chogoria, Meru, Nanyuki, Timau, Naro Moru, or any of the other small towns surrounding Mount Kenya, it's extremely easy to get a *matatu* to the next town, or back to Nairobi.

Most *matatu*s heading out of Nairobi in any direction leave town from the River Road/Accra Road area, on the northeast side of town. Sometimes, catching one is a matter of walking around and finding one with a sign in the window indicating it's going to the town you're going to.

Renting a Car

Do not rent a car for either Kilimanjaro or Mount Kenya!

On Kilimanjaro, outfitters provide transportation to and from the trailhead, so it is totally unnecessary to rent a car. Besides, if you rent one, you'll have to leave it at a trailhead, then make sure you come back out of the park via that trailhead. The best aspect of climbing Kilimanjaro is going up one route and down another so you get to see a completely

Porters weighing loads at the Marangu Gate, Kilimanjaro
(Photo © Cameron M. Burns)

different aspect of the mountain. Also, if you leave a rented vehicle in any of the small villages around Kilimanjaro for five nights, it's likely you'll owe the rental agency a new car by the time you get off the mountain.

Mount Kenya is the same. Leave a car at a trailhead and you'll likely find parts missing, vandalism, or the entire vehicle stolen. To get around Mount Kenya, any of the outfitters listed in the appendix can help you arrange transportation.

Still, if you must rent a car, it's fairly easy. There are big rental agencies in Nairobi, Dar, and Mombasa, as well as all the smaller towns in the country. Even in the smallest village, it's usually easy to find someone who will rent you a vehicle, even though they might not be part of an official rental agency. Rates vary wildly, but plan on spending at the very least US$100/day. The cheapest I've found was US$80 a day for an absolute junker.

KILIMANJARO REGULATIONS AND FEES

Kilimanjaro is very much a "package tour" mountain, and you're going to end up as part of a group, large or small, whether you like it or not.

The most immediate reason for the package tour status is that Kilimanjaro National Park (KINAPA) regulations require you to climb the mountain with a Tanzanian guide or outfitter. No independent climbing is allowed. You must travel with a registered guide in the park at all times, whether you're going 1 meter inside the park gate or doing a serious technical mountaineering route that will take days.

Although this package tour mentality might sound restrictive, it has several benefits, the most important being that you'll save hundreds of dollars and dozens of hours of frustration that would be required to organize food, transportation, porters, and park permits if you did the mountain independently.

In addition, KINAPA also requires that you hire at least one porter to carry the guide's belongings. You are allowed to carry your own food and equipment, if you choose, but since porters are about the cheapest part of an ascent (US$1 to $2 per porter per day), you're better off hiring some for yourself as well. Two to three porters per climber is standard. The porters will take a load off your back and make your ascent an extremely enjoyable experience.

Your outfitter will arrange a guide and porters for you. (See list of Kilimanjaro outfitters in Appendix A.)

There is one other regulation you should be aware of: KINAPA does not allow children under age ten to go higher than 2,700 meters (9,000 feet) on the mountain. Right or wrong, park officials fear children this young might be severely affected by the altitude.

Climbing Reservations

Besides guides and at least one porter, a reservation is required to climb any route on the mountain. KINAPA limits the number of non-Tanzanian climbers to fifty-eight people per day on the Marangu Route, plus thirty-two more on the other routes combined. Your outfitter will arrange a reservation for you at park headquarters either the day you begin your ascent or, if it's in high season, possibly a day or two before.

These mountain reservations get filled up fairly quickly, so you should organize a climb with an outfitter as soon as you get to Arusha, Moshi, or Marangu. Reservations made through big tour operators in Europe and North America work fine, but you will pay a premium for booking from overseas. (See Avoiding Rip-offs in Chapter 2.)

Technical Mountaineering Reservations

Climbing any route on Kili besides the standard trekking routes requires an additional reservation at park headquarters in Marangu. Whereas literally anyone who has the money to pay for a trekking route on the mountain is allowed to go up, technical mountaineers must make a formal application with the park to do mountaineering routes. For obvious reasons, KINAPA officials don't like to let unqualified climbers try routes that are beyond their abilities.

To make the application, KINAPA recommends sending a letter describing your proposed climb, along with a resume of your climbing record, to the park warden at P.O. Box 96, Marangu, Tanzania. KINAPA officials will then ascertain whether you are qualified for a technical mountaineering route. Few are ever turned down.

If you send a letter from home to Africa to let KINAPA know you're coming, more than likely you will not get a response. I've sent several letters over the years and never received a reply. The best thing to do is to send a letter a few weeks before you leave for Africa so park officials know you're coming. Then arrange to meet with them once you are at park headquarters in Marangu.

Perhaps the strangest aspect of technical mountaineering on Kilimanjaro is that although you are required to hire a guide when you go inside the park—as you are on trekking routes—most local guides have no technical mountaineering experience. Therefore they will guide you to the base of your proposed route, leave you there, then walk around and meet you on the summit. The park does not require the guides to go with technical mountaineers on their proposed routes.

One other climbing regulation: electric power drills (for bolting) and leaving fixed ropes and other technical gear after an ascent are not allowed. Park philosophy is that fixed ropes—if left permanently—create visual impacts.

Hut Reservations

You will need hut reservations only for the huts on the Marangu Route. The huts on the other routes (Mweka, Umbwe, Machame, Shira Plateau—there are none on the Rongai Route) are merely burned-out metal shells filled with trash, food scraps, and firewood. Most non-Tanzanians who use these other routes bring a tent, and the huts are used only by the guides and porters, who don't seem to mind their state of disrepair. If you do decide to use the huts on these other routes, it's a matter of first come, first served.

If you do not have a tent and really must stay in huts as you ascend the mountain, the ones on the Marangu Route are in fairly good condition. There are three main huts (Mandara Hut, Horombo Hut, and Kibo Hut), spaced a day's walk apart. However, each of these huts is surrounded by a virtual village of buildings, and the names refer to the old huts that existed long before the other structures were built. Some of the additional buildings are for porters and guides to sleep in, others are for park officials, others for small shops. Tourists generally sleep in the original huts.

At the time of this writing, an overnight stay in one of the huts on the Marangu Route cost US$40 per person per night; reservations must be made at the park offices at the Marangu Gate. Your outfitter will arrange these reservations for you as part of your climb.

When you arrive at each hut complex on the Marangu Route, you must go straight to the caretaker's office and show your reservations to park officials, who will help you find your hut and sleeping quarters. As with most other things, your guide will take care of this for you.

There are no facilities in the huts except for bunks, so you will need to bring a sleeping bag and sleeping pad. Cooking must be done outside. At both Horombo and Mandara Huts, there are separate facilities for washing—small bathroom buildings, with cold showers and toilets.

The toilets at Kibo Hut are like toilets on other routes on the mountain—big earthen pits. There is no natural water supply at Kibo Hut, so there are no showers.

Fees

The fees for just about anything on Kilimanjaro are steep, steeper than most of the routes in Africa. In January 1997, they went up by 50 percent, making even very recent guidebooks out of date. The reliance on national parks for general government revenues in Africa also means that fees will likely continue to rise every other year or so.

As of March 1997, KINAPA fees were as follows:

Entrance fee: US$25 per person per day

Guide/porter entrance fee: US$5 per person per trip up the mountain

Camping fee: US$50 per person per day

Hut fee: US$40 per person per day

Rescue fee deposit (for technical mountaineering only): US$250, $200 of which will be returned to you after your climb if you have not used rescue services (the unreturned $50 goes into rescue team supplies and training)

Rescue fee (for everyone): US$20 per person per trip up the mountain

Discuss with your outfitter at the time you make your reservation exactly how the park fees will be paid. Because most Tanzanian outfitters are always strapped for cash, it is common for them to get you to pay park fees for the whole trip when you show up at the Marangu Gate. (If you are doing the paying, bring U.S. dollars or traveler's checks.)

If you are paying park fees yourself, they need to be deducted from the overall costs of your climb. If you are climbing a route other than the Marangu Route, your outfitter will usually add the park fees into the cost of a climb and send a runner to Marangu to pay them on your behalf.

MOUNT KENYA REGULATIONS AND FEES

Mount Kenya National Park is much more like national parks found in the United States and other Western countries and is well suited to "independent" or self-created climbing excursions.

Regulations

The regulations for Mount Kenya are pretty straightforward and are posted at every park gate:

- All visitors must sign in when they enter the park and sign out when they leave. All visitors must pay the daily park entrance fee.
- No harassing the wildlife.
- All litter must be carried out (you might be asked to show your litter at the gate when leaving the park).
- Driving within the park is prohibited after 6:00 P.M. (dark).
- No one is allowed to enter the park alone.
- No parasailing is allowed in the park.

No technical mountaineering or trekking permits are required. You must only pay the park entrance fee and the camping fees (see Fees, below). Unlike Kilimanjaro, guides and porters are not required on Mount Kenya. About the only regulation of consequence for most visitors is that you are not allowed to enter the park alone.

Mount Kenya National Park will not refund daily park entrance and camping fees if you leave the park earlier than you expect. And if you stay longer than expected within the park, you must pay for the additional days and nights on your way out.

Hut Reservations

There are both large bunkhouses and smaller huts on Mount Kenya. The majority of these buildings are privately owned by various groups.

On the Naro Moru Route, the bunkhouses at the Meteorological Station ("Met Station") and Mackinder's Camp are administered by the Naro Moru River Lodge; space can be reserved through the lodge (see Appendix A for address). The cost is around US$10 per night.

The Old Moses and Shipton's Camp bunkhouses on the Sirimon Route are administered by the Mountain Rock Lodge; reservations can be made through the lodge (see Appendix A for address). The cost is also around US$10 per night. If the bunkhouses are not full, it's possible to show up and simply arrange a sleeping space upon your arrival.

Other huts on the mountain are on a first-come, first-served basis. The various organizations responsible for the huts—like the Mountain Club of Kenya—no longer actively collect hut fees.

At both the bunkhouses and the huts, you will find plenty of local porters and guides who will offer to take your money so they can pay the organizations that own the huts. Don't pay them!

Because of the hassle of dealing with huts, bookings, and fees, I thoroughly advocate bringing a tent and camping instead.

Fees

The fees for Mount Kenya aren't as steep as they are for Kilimanjaro, but they still hurt if you're on a budget. As of March 1997, they were as follows:

> Entrance fee: US$15 per day for day visitors; US$10 per day for climbers
>
> Guide/porter park entrance fee: US$2 per person per day
>
> Camping fee: US$8 per person per day
>
> Hut fee: US$8 to $10 per night

CONSERVATION

The old adage "Pack it in, pack it out" applies as much on Kilimanjaro and Mount Kenya as any other mountain in the world. Perhaps especially here, as guides and porters—who, not surprisingly, grow tired of lugging tourists and their stuff around—often dump trash in heaps out back of huts, through the floors of huts, and next to camping areas on both mountains.

Make sure that after any meal or overnight camp that all your refuse is collected and carried along for the remainder of the trip. Guides and porters will often let their packs be loaded with refuse, only to sneak it out and toss it aside when you aren't looking. If need be, carry the refuse yourself.

Mount Kenya National Park requires that trekkers and technical mountaineers show their trash on the way out of the park, although often the rule is not enforced. Although Kilimanjaro does not yet have a trash policy, it is likely just a matter of time before one is created since the trash situation there is miles worse than on Mount Kenya. On the other hand, Kilimanjaro National Park does official cleanups on the mountain several times a year (although it's hard to believe).

Evacuation and urination should be done in only designated pit toilets, which are at all overnight camping areas on the mountain. If you are on the trail between overnight stops, make sure you eliminate at least 100 meters from any watercourse.

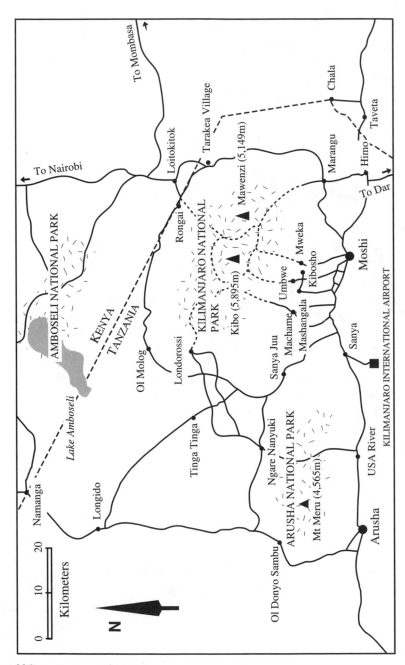

Kilimanjaro and vicinity

CHAPTER 4

KILIMANJARO

*There, ahead, all he could see, as wide as all the world, great,
high, and unbelievably white in the sun, was the square top
of Kilimanjaro.*
—Ernest Hemingway, *The Snows of Kilimanjaro*

Kilimanjaro. There are few mountains in the world whose name evokes
as much passion, wonder, and awe. From Ernest Hemingway's famous
short story to the classic John Wayne film *Hatari!*, Kilimanjaro has always held a unique place in both the Western and African psyche. When
you get to Kili, you'll realize why.

It is often said that Kilimanjaro is the biggest freestanding mountain in the world, in that it is not connected to other peaks in a range.
Rising dramatically more than 5,000 meters above the East African plain
(itself 800 meters above sea level), the massif is 60 kilometers long and
40 kilometers wide. It lies about 330 kilometers south of the equator,
wholly within the United Republic of Tanzania.

Kilimanjaro is a complex mountain. The name *Kilimanjaro* actually
refers to an entire massif comprised of three separate extinct volcanoes:
Kibo (5,895 meters/19,341 feet), Mawenzi (5,149 meters/16,893 feet),
and Shira (3,962 meters/12,999 feet). To confuse matters, the summit
of Kibo is often referred to as Uhuru Peak (5,895 meters/19,341 feet)
(formerly Kaiser Wilhelm Spitze), and the highest point on Mawenzi is
called Hans Meyer Peak.

Because of the mountain's proximity to both the equator and the
Indian Ocean and because of its tremendous height, Kilimanjaro boasts

five major ecological zones, each of which occupies about 1,000 meters of altitude: the lower slopes (800 to 1,800 meters); the montane forest zone (1,800 to 2,700 meters); the heath and moorland zone (2,700 to 4,000 meters); the alpine desert zone (4,000 to 5,000 meters); and the summit zone (5,000 to 5,895 meters). Each is a world in itself, with unique flora and fauna found in few other places in Africa.

In the early 1900s, the area around Kilimanjaro was established as a game preserve. In 1921, the Tanganyikan government changed that status to a forest and game preserve. In 1957, Tanganyika National Parks authorities, with support from many local and international conservation groups, formally proposed creating a national park that would include the mountain and the surrounding forest and game preserve.

It took until 1973 for the formal creation of Kilimanjaro National Park (KINAPA). Its boundaries were based on a fairly simple concept: any land above the 2,700-meter level is in the park. Altogether, the park comprises 756 square kilometers.

Kilimanjaro National Park was officially opened in 1977, and in 1989 it was also declared a world heritage site by the World Heritage Convention.

THE NAME

Kilimanjaro's name has been a source of speculation for years. The Wachagga people of northern Tanzania—who emigrated to the Kilimanjaro area 250 to 300 years ago—claim to have no name for the entire mountain but are believed to be responsible for the individual names of Kipoo (Kibo) and Kimawenzi (Mawenzi).

Most historians and anthropologists believe the first part of the word *Kilimanjaro*—*kilima*—is a corruption of the Swahili word for "mountain"—*mlima*. However, the prefix *ki* is confusing because in Swahili, the addition of *ki* makes a noun diminutive, so *kilima* means "small mountain." Many believe the diminutive reference is one of affection for the mountain.

The second part of the word—*njaro*—is open to much greater speculation. Some believe *njaro* is derived from the Swahili word *ngara,* which means "to shine." Others believe it comes from the Wachagga word for caravan, since in the early days of East Africa exploration, caravans used the mountain as a landmark.

Some believe *njaro* refers to a demon who was thought by coastal residents to cause cold. Still others believe that *njaro* is a corruption of

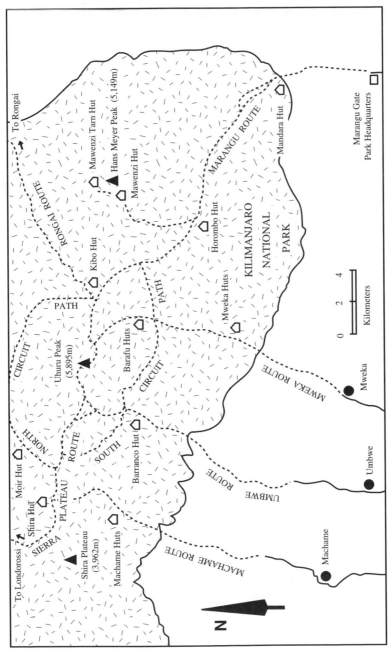

Overview of Kilimanjaro

the Masai word for water, *ngare,* since Kilimanjaro is a water source for much of the Masai territory that lies north and east of it.

POPULARITY

Kilimanjaro is one of the most popular mountains in the world. In 1982, 4,600 nonresidents and 1,600 residents visited Kilimanjaro National Park. By 1991, the number of nonresident visitors had gone up to 10,800, while the number of resident visitors had decreased to 810.

Of the 10,800 nonresidents who visited KINAPA in 1991, 9,800 attempted to climb the Marangu/Normal Route to the summit, and about 1,000 took other routes. In 1994–95 (the latest numbers available), the park recorded a total of 14,578 visitors.

It is estimated that only 40 to 50 percent of all summit-bound climbers are successful in reaching Uhuru Peak.

In 1991, the park earned US$1.75 million from park fees. Reportedly the money goes into much more than maintaining the park, but to KINAPA's credit, it does cleanups on the trashed-out Marangu Route twice a year.

In January 1997, park fees jumped by 50 percent. Similarly large increases should be expected in the future as East African nations tap into the growing worldwide tourism boom.

WILDLIFE SIGHTINGS

Although the wildlife you will see on Kilimanjaro won't compare to the wildlife you'll find on safari in East African game parks, the mountain is still home to many exotic creatures (see Wildlife, in Chapter 2). Dik-dik, duikers, bushbucks, blue monkeys, colobus monkeys, chameleons, mongeese, and sunbirds are all part of the average ascent.

The College of African Wildlife Management, located in Mweka Village, appreciates any reports of animal sightings you might experience on Kilimanjaro. To report sightings, write: College of African Wildlife Management, P.O. Box 3031, Moshi, Tanzania.

GEOGRAPHY

Although geographically, Kilimanjaro is very easy to understand, the way the routes are named is not. The half-dozen forest and moorland approach routes that penetrate the forest and moorland areas (Marangu,

Mweka, Umbwe, Machame, Shira Plateau, and Rongai) and the way those routes connect to routes that climb the final 1,200 meters of the mountain can be extremely confusing for the first-time visitor.

All these forest and moorland routes get to about the 3,500–4,500 meter level, then join the South Circuit Path. They do not go to the summit. From the South Circuit Path, various walking, scrambling, and technical mountaineering routes then lead to the summit.

Trekkers usually climb the final 1,200 meters to the summit by one of the three easiest routes up Kibo: the Normal Route, the Barafu Route, or the Western Breach Route. Technical mountaineers can choose other routes. Discuss which summit route you want to take with your outfitter before you leave Moshi, since the company must make the appropriate arrangements with KINAPA.

The names of combination routes on Kilimanjaro are also extremely confusing because the names don't completely describe where the routes go. For instance, the popular Machame–Mweka Route isn't just a combination of the Machame and Mweka forest/moorland routes. The climb begins with the Machame Route, then takes in a part of the Shira Plateau Route, some of the South Circuit Path, then climbs the final section of Kibo via the Barafu Route. It then descends the Barafu Route to Barafu Huts before joining the Mweka Route to descend through the forest.

Likewise, the Rongai Route ascends through the forest, but at Kibo Hut, where the Rongai Route ends, climbers usually take the Normal Route to the summit. To confuse matters, the Normal Route is often referred to as the Marangu Route because it joins up neatly with the Marangu Route.

The best thing to do is study a map, which will sort out much of the confusion. Actually getting on the mountain will sort it out even more.

One reason these forest and moorland routes are arranged in combinations is because the Umbwe and Mweka Routes are so steep and rough that they are incredibly difficult to ascend. Most outfitters prefer to use them only for descents. If you're so inclined, you can easily arrange ascents of these two routes, but tip your guide and porters well!

FOREST / MOORLAND ROUTES

The following route descriptions begin with the ever-popular Marangu Route, then move clockwise around the mountain through the southern glaciers to the Breach Wall and the northern glaciers, which lie on the western and northern side of Kibo.

A note about descents on the forest/moorland routes: The descriptions here—with details on elevation gain, time to travel between huts, and so forth—are for ascent only. On the descent, you will travel much more quickly and generally skip every other hut. For example, on the Marangu/Normal Route, after a night at Kibo Hut and a climb to Uhuru Peak in the morning, it is customary to descend to Horombo Hut that afternoon for one night, followed by a descent to the park gate the next day.

MARANGU ROUTE

Among the porters of Marangu Village the Marangu Route is known as the Coca-Cola Route. Like the beverage, it's highly popular. Probably 90 percent of all Kili climbers follow it. It's also the cheapest product around.

Although the Marangu Route is often criticized as being "the most crowded route" and a "bad experience," it's actually very beautiful and doesn't deserve its tourist-route reputation. One of the best things about the Marangu Route is that it's possible to stay in huts all the way up the mountain, and there are facilities for bathing (that is, cold water) at Mandara and Horombo Huts. The other benefit is that mineral water, beer, and Coke are available at all the main huts (Mandara, Horombo, Kibo), although you can expect to pay more than double what these products would cost down in Moshi.

The Marangu Route starts at the Marangu Gate, several kilometers above the village of the same name.

To reach Marangu, drive east from Moshi on the main Arusha–Taveta Road for 27 kilometers to the bustling roadside village of Himo. Between Moshi and Himo are some of Tanzania's biggest baobab trees. The logs hanging from various trees are locally constructed beehives.

The signed turnoff to Dar, on the right, is shortly before Himo. At Himo, turn left (north) and continue about 14 kilometers to the village of Marangu. This road is paved all the way, a reflection of the economic impact of the Marangu Route. The town of Marangu is spread out along the road. The Marangu Hotel—a popular place for climbers—is on the left. At the Y intersection in Marangu (the only intersection in town, lying near the post office), veer left, toward the Capricorn Hotel. Continue about 5 kilometers up the paved road to KINAPA's Marangu Gate, at about 1,900 meters elevation.

Here, either you or your guide will have to pay park fees and check in, which can take anywhere from 10 minutes to an hour.

Once the park formalities have been dealt with, the walking begins.

In the following descriptions, the trails have been broken down into segments that most parties travel in a day.

MARANGU ROUTE: MARANGU GATE TO MANDARA HUT / DAY 1

Ascent: 1,900 meters to 2,700 meters
Distance: 8 kilometers
Time: 3 to 4 hours

From the park gate, the trail winds up through the forest on a paved road that quickly gives way to a wide dirt road. After 10 minutes of walking, a subsidiary trail branches off to the left. This trail joins the main trail higher up, and is much narrower, but many use it hoping to see more wildlife than on the main trail. You'll likely see just as much wildlife on the main path.

The main trail gradually narrows as it climbs through the forest toward Mandara Hut and is no more than a single-file track in some places. Mandara Hut is just one of many A-frame huts clustered together in the forest at 2,700 meters. This is the standard first-night stopping point on the Marangu Route, and the huts can accommodate dozens of people. There are many blue monkeys in the surrounding forest. If you get to camp early, wander up the trail toward Horombo Hut a few minutes and you'll likely see them in the lush vegetation.

MARANGU ROUTE: MANDARA HUT TO HOROMBO HUT / DAY 2

Ascent: 2,700 meters to 3,700 meters
Distance: 11 kilometers
Time: 5 to 7 hours

From Mandara Hut the trail continues northwest through the forest. A few minutes up the path, a trail going left leads to the Maundi Crater, a rounded knob rising above the forest that offers spectacular views. It is possible to take this trail, then rejoin the main trail higher up the mountain.

Just after the Maundi Crater, the trail enters a badly burned area that dates from a massive fire that burned about 200,000 acres of land on the southeast side of the mountain in January 1997.

The trail to Horombo Hut is well marked, and there are only short steep sections where the trail dips across creeks. The views of Kibo and Mawenzi are inspirational.

Like Mandara Hut, there is an entire village of huts around Horombo Hut (3,700 meters), with a camping area on the hillside above. A clear stream runs through the complex (but its water should be treated before use). Many parties spend only one night at Horombo, but if you think you might have trouble with altitude higher up the mountain, it's best to spend two nights. Arrange the extra night with your outfitter before you start up the mountain.

If you are headed to Mawenzi, the trail to Mawenzi Hut intersects the main Marangu Route trail just above the Horombo Hut camping area. From this point, it's about 2 to 3 hours to Mawenzi Hut.

MARANGU ROUTE: HOROMBO HUT TO KIBO HUT / DAY 3

Ascent: 3,700 meters to 4,700 meters
Distance: 11 kilometers
Time: 5 to 6 hours

The trail above Horombo Hut is well marked. After an hour's hike, at 4,000 meters the trail crosses the Maua River, a good place to get water.

Horombo Hut area, Marangu Route, Kilimanjaro
(Photo © Cameron M. Burns)

Cutting the ice window, Christmas 1981, Mount Kenya
(Photo © Lindsay Griffin)

William Sandy below the summit ice field, Kilimanjaro
(Photo © Cameron M. Burns)

Overleaf: Mount Kenya (Photo © Doug Scott)

Benny Bach on Southeast Gully, Point John
(Photo © Cameron M. Burns)

Arrow Glacier Hut (Photo © Cameron M. Burns)

P. Cummings approaching Firmin's Tower, Mount Kenya
(Photo © Bart O'Brien)

Descending on the east side of Lava Tower en route to Barranco Hut
(Photo © Cameron M. Burns)

Waterfall near Chogoria Route roadhead, Mount Kenya
(Photo © Cameron M. Burns)

Giant groundsel with Mawenzi in the background
(Photo © Cameron M. Burns)

Elephant skull, Burguret Route, Mount Kenya
(Photo © Cameron M. Burns)

Climbing toward Shipton's Notch, West Ridge, Mount Kenya
(Photo © Bart O'Brien)

Second cave, Rongai Route, Kilimanjaro (Photo ©Cameron M. Burns)

Next page: Tut Braithwaite climbing the direct start to the Breach Wall Direct
(Photo © Doug Scott)

The official last water point on the Marangu Route lies a short walk farther up the trail and is well marked with two signs. However, it is a small, muddy creek with not much to recommend it.

About an hour beyond "last water," a sign indicates that the trail is entering the Saddle—the area between Mawenzi and Kibo. Near the Saddle sign, the South Circuit Path takes off to the left (southwest). The trail junction is not very prominent, and the Saddle sign is the best way to tell you've reached it. (From here, one can follow the South Circuit Path around the southern side of the mountain. This is a fairly straight-forward way of accessing the southern glacier routes—the Rebmann, Decken, Kersten, and Heim Glaciers—on Kibo.)

Continuing straight, the Marangu route crosses the Saddle and heads toward Kibo, reaching Kibo Hut at 4,700 meters. Like the other overnight stops on the Marangu Route, the Kibo Hut area is a collection of huts. Kibo Hut itself has about a half-dozen rooms, each with eight to fifteen bunks. From Kibo Hut, the Normal Route (also known as the Marangu Route) on Kibo leads to the crater rim at Gillman's Point and the summit. (See the Kibo section, below, for a description of the Normal Route from Kibo Hut to the summit.)

MWEKA ROUTE

The Mweka Route is steep and rough. Most outfitters and guides consider it a descent route only, although you can ascend it. It is the most direct way of getting to the Barafu Route and the Rebmann Glacier on Kibo.

The route starts at the Mweka Gate, on the Mweka Road, located 13 kilometers north of Moshi.

MWEKA ROUTE: MWEKA GATE TO MWEKA HUTS / DAY 1

> **Ascent:** 1,500 meters to 3,100 meters
> **Distance:** 10 kilometers
> **Time:** 4 to 5 hours

From the Mweka Gate, the route follows an old logging road for several kilometers, then goes for several kilometers on a narrow, often muddy track that is extremely uneven and slippery in places.

The trail continues along a ridge between two valleys before emerging at Mweka Huts (3,100 meters) after about 10 kilometers. The two huts are Uniports, like most huts on Kilimanjaro. There is water in a small valley 5 minutes to the southeast. This is the last water on the Mweka Route.

MWEKA ROUTE: MWEKA HUTS TO BARAFU HUTS / DAY 2

Ascent: 3,100 meters to 4,600 meters
Distance: 11 kilometers
Time: 6 to 8 hours

Above Mweka Huts, the trail winds its way up a rocky rib before emerging in the alpine desert on the eastern rib of the Southeast Valley.

After you cross the South Circuit Path, it is about 2 kilometers to Barafu Huts. (From Barafu Huts to the summit, see the description for Barafu Route in the Kibo section.)

UMBWE ROUTE

This route is easily one of the best experiences of a lifetime. It is breathtaking, wild, rough, and extremely steep. It displays Kilimanjaro's wildly dramatic geological formations better than any other route on the mountain. And almost no one goes up this route.

Like the Mweka Route, the Umbwe Route is generally considered a descent route. Some tour operators might decline an ascent of this route, or charge you a lot extra.

There are several roads from Moshi to Umbwe Village. The best way to get there is to drive west from Moshi on the Moshi–Arusha Road, and turn right on the Lyamungu Road. At the T intersection, turn right toward Mango, cross the Sere River, then turn left, past the Umbwe mission and school. A few kilometers further up the road lies the park gate.

UMBWE ROUTE: UMBWE GATE TO CAMP I / DAY 1

Ascent: 1,400 meters to 3,000 meters
Distance: 11 kilometers
Time: 5 to 6 hours

From the gate at 1,400 meters, the trail winds up through the forest, following a ridge between two deep valleys. In many places it is necessary to pull yourself up on tree roots and branches. At around 3,000 meters, you will reach a small clearing and cave. This is generally the first night's camp, commonly called Camp I. There are campsites on the small hill above the cave, as well as right in front of it, and there are several obvious water sources around the cave.

UMBWE ROUTE: CAMP 1 TO BARRANCO HUT / DAY 2

Ascent: 3,000 meters to 3,900 meters
Distance: 7 kilometers
Time: 4 to 5 hours

The trail continues up the ridge, getting steeper and more interesting as it progresses up the mountain. In some places, the trail wanders along ledges with 600-meter drops on either side.

At about the 3,200-meter level, it is necessary to climb a short (10-meter) rock cliff. This cliff is only a scramble (American Class 3), and there is little exposure, but it requires climbing rock and pulling your way up a few branches and roots. Most visitors to Kilimanjaro who have never climbed rock have no problem with this section of the route.

The trail continues up the ridge, which gets increasingly easier and wider before arriving at Barranco Hut, where the trail joins the South Circuit Path.

Once at Barranco Hut, you can opt for either the Western Breach Route or the Barafu Route (if you're hiking) to the summit of Kibo, or you can do one of the southern glacier routes (technical mountaineering). (See the Kibo section.)

MACHAME ROUTE

While the Marangu Route is dubbed the Coca-Cola Route, the Machame Route is known as the Whiskey Route. It's more expensive to ascend, and its fantastic views are much more intoxicating.

Like other forest routes on this side of Kili, the Machame Route is generally considered an ascent route. When combined with the Barafu Route on Kibo to the summit and the Mweka Route as a descent through the forest (also known as the Machame–Mweka Route), it is easily the best forest/moorland route for acclimatization on Kilimanjaro, as well as one of the most scenic outings on the mountain.

It climbs slowly through the forest before emerging on the edge of the Shira Plateau and joining the Shira Plateau Route, then traverses the mountain, taking in the South Circuit Path, with overnight stops at Barranco Hut and Barafu Huts before a slow grind up Kibo to the summit. Because of the slow ascent, this combination route has the highest rate of success of any route on the mountain.

The Machame Route, by itself, is also the second most beautiful route on the mountain after the Umbwe Route. It starts above the village of Machame, on the southwestern slopes of Kilimanjaro. Like most villages in Africa, Machame has no real center but is strung along the road for several kilometers. To reach the village, drive west on the Arusha–Moshi Road from Moshi for 13 kilometers, then turn right onto the Machame Road (signed) and drive another about 7 kilometers. When you reach the village market, veer left between the buildings. Another few kilometers of steep dirt road will lead to the well-marked Machame Gate.

MACHAME ROUTE: MACHAME GATE TO MACHAME HUTS / DAY 1

Ascent: 1,800 meters to 3,000 meters
Distance: 10 kilometers
Time: 5 to 6 hours

The trail bypasses the park offices to the left (west), then follows a four-wheel-drive road for several kilometers before it begins thinning to a narrow jungle track that follows a ridge. The trail is well used, so losing it is not an issue. Five to 6 hours of hiking brings you to Machame Huts, at 3,000 meters. Like nearly all the huts on Kili—except those on the Marangu Route—they are Uniports in a state of disrepair. There are good camping sites on the hillside above the huts (to the east), and fresh water is available from the creek down the steep hill behind the huts to the northwest.

MACHAME ROUTE: MACHAME HUTS TO SHIRA HUT / DAY 2

Ascent: 3,000 meters to 3,800 meters
Distance: 7 kilometers
Time: 5 hours

From Machame Huts, the trail enters the moorlands and more or less follows a fin of volcanic rock protruding from the mountain. About 2 hours from Machame Huts, the trail reaches a semicircular rock wall that must be negotiated. The wall is a scramble (American Class 3), but it is short (8 meters), and exposure is not a problem. The average person—with no climbing experience whatsoever—can manage it. Above the wall is a scenic rest stop.

Next, the trail heads northwest, away from Kibo, and crosses two streams before emerging on the Shira Plateau, near Shira Cave. Shira Hut lies a few hundred meters to the northwest. Most parties camp near the cave, as Shira Hut is old and dirty.

At this point, the Machame Route has joined the Shira Plateau Route. (See Shira Plateau Route, below.)

SHIRA PLATEAU ROUTE

To reach the trailhead for the Shira Plateau Route, drive west from Moshi on the Arusha–Moshi Road for 26 kilometers, then turn right (north) for 22 kilometers to the town of Sanya Juu. Often your guide will stop in Sanya Juu for last-minute supplies or lunch. From Sanya Juu, it's another 40 kilometers or so to Londorossi, and the roads get progressively worse. To the first-time visitor, Londorossi looks like a town straight out of a Hollywood Western. It is constructed entirely of wood, and its dirt streets conjure up images of Tombstone. It's easy to go the wrong way in Londorossi, but watch for signs pointing to the Londorossi Gate.

It's possible to drive the 11 kilometers from the gate all the way to the trailhead at 3,500 meters; however, the road is extremely rough. (There are no facilities at the trailhead except an outhouse-style toilet.)

SHIRA PLATEAU ROUTE: SHIRA PLATEAU ROUTE TRAILHEAD TO SHIRA HUT / DAY 1
Ascent: 3,500 meters to 3,800 meters
Distance: 6 kilometers
Time: 4 hours

From the trailhead, the trail goes east, breaking out across the center of the Shira Plateau. About 3 to 4 hours' walk from the trailhead, you will reach Shira Hut. There are many campsites within the first few kilometers along the Shira Plateau Route, and a late start from Moshi often necessitates camping before reaching Shira Hut.

Shira Cave lies another 20 minutes' walk to the south-southeast of Shira Hut. Most parties camp here rather than at Shira Hut, which is old and dirty. There is camping near the cave (about 5 minutes' walk to the west-southwest of the cave), where a second large cave often serves as a kitchen/campsite for porters and guides. There is a tremendous pile of garbage at this camp, and at night, dozens of dik-dik roam about, picking at the mess. Camping in the Shira Cave is prohibited. There is a wooden toilet building next to it.

Water is available from several sources. If you've come up the Machame Route, there are two creeks back along the Machame Route, toward Machame Huts. The first stream is about a 10-minute walk from Shira Cave. A closer water source is a creek about 300 meters directly west of Shira Cave. Sometimes, however, this creek dries out.

From Shira Hut, it is possible to go in several different directions: to Lava Tower Hut, to Moir Hut, or to Barranco Hut. That's because just east of Shira Hut, the Shira Plateau trail meets the North Circuit Path, which gives numerous options.

Because most climbers who use the Shira Plateau trail (or portions of it) are either headed for the Western Breach Route on Kibo or doing the Machame–Mweka combination route, those two sections of trail are covered below.

Shira Plateau Route: Shira Hut to Arrow Glacier Hut / Day 2, Option 1

Ascent: 3,800 meters to 4,800 meters
Distance: 6 kilometers
Time: 3 to 4 hours

From the Shira Cave area, the Shira Plateau trail skirts right (south) of the cave and then follows a long, low, thin fin of rock for several kilometers before it slowly trends southeast, aiming for a striking tower of rock, Lava Tower. About halfway between Shira Cave and Lava Tower, the North and South Circuit Paths join the Shira Plateau trail. The junction is not well marked. In fact, the only indication that you have intersected the North and South Circuit Paths is some red spray paint on a rock stating "Moya Hut" (Moir Hut).

At this point, you can follow the North Circuit Path left (north) to Moir Hut or the South Circuit Path right (south) to Barranco Hut, or you can go straight, which takes you toward Lava Tower Hut and the trail up to Arrow Glacier Hut.

After intersecting with the North and South Circuit Paths, the Shira Plateau trail flattens out a little bit and continues east-southeast to Lava Tower.

Just after the intersection, the trail crosses a fairly deep valley, and climbing out of it is a grind. Above this hill, the path crosses two broad, flat valleys before reaching Lava Tower Hut (4,500 meters). The hut is a ruin, and the area is rarely used for camping.

Lava Tower Hut is the access point for the Western Breach area (also known as the Arrow Glacier area) and the Western Breach Route. Just east of Lava Tower, the small trail to Arrow Glacier Hut angles off up the hill to the northeast. It's a couple of hours' walk to Arrow Glacier Hut (4,800 meters), which is nothing more than a ruin.

Shira Plateau Route: Shira Hut to Barranco Hut / Day 2, Option 2

Ascent: 3,800 meters to 3,900 meters
Distance: 10 kilometers
Time: 5 to 6 hours

There are two ways of getting to Barranco Hut from Shira Hut. Each offers a different way to go around Lava Tower.

The first way is to follow the trail described above, which leads to Lava Tower Hut. From Lava Tower Hut, stay on the main trail as it descends east and south around Lava Tower. The trail to Arrow Glacier Hut will go up the steep hill to the left. This route around Lava Tower is highly recommended as it aids in acclimatization and is very scenic.

The other way is to follow the Shira Plateau trail east, toward the intersection with the North and South Circuit Paths (see Day 2, Option 1, above), then go south and east on the South Circuit Path, around the south side of Lava Tower.

Both routes around Lava Tower join up east of Lava Tower and continue down a beautiful valley to the Barranco Wall area and Barranco Hut, another dirty metal shell.

Rongai Route

The Rongai Route is a very different experience from the routes on the southwest side of the mountain. It's drier, it's covered with tall grass and elephant scat (and the elephants that produced the scat), and there are no huts. The best thing about the Rongai Route is that it offers spectacular views out over the broad, flat Masai lands north of the Tanzania-Kenya border. These sweeping views give one a feel for what being on a high mountain in East Africa is really all about.

The Rongai Route is currently the standard route on the north side of Kilimanjaro. Getting to the trailhead requires driving along the Tanzania-Kenya border.

To reach the trailhead, drive through the village of Marangu, veer right at the Marangu Post Office, then traverse around the entire eastern side of the mountain by way of several small, but interesting villages. The road is wildly rough!

The Tanzania-Kenya border is on the north side of Tarakea Village, which lies on the northeastern side of the Kilimanjaro massif. Instead of driving through the border gate into Kenya, take the road to Rongai, which leads off to the left just before the gate. After many kilometers, the wooden town of Rongai is reached. A stop at the park gate (up the road to the left a short distance from Rongai) is required before you can begin hiking. Then it's necessary to drive back down to Rongai and continue left around the mountain for several more kilometers, to a turnout area on the left, where a big white metal sign proclaims the virtues of the "Snow-Cap Mountain Climbing Camp—Rongai."

RONGAI ROUTE: RONGAI ROUTE TRAILHEAD TO FIRST CAVE / DAY 1

Ascent: 2,000 meters to 2,880 meters
Distance: 8 kilometers
Time: 4 to 5 hours

From the trailhead, the route follows an old four-wheel-drive road as it winds through the forest for about 1.5 kilometers of jungle before emerging in the heather at about 2,500 meters. The trail is not at all steep, but is rather a gentle hike through beautiful country. There are tons (literally) of elephant manure on this section of the trail. The first night's camp is at First Cave, at about 2,880 meters. You'll find some excellent campsites just above First Cave with breathtaking views over the plains to the north. There are a toilet structure and a wooden table with benches, but no hut. Water is just down the trail below First Cave.

RONGAI ROUTE: FIRST CAVE TO THIRD CAVE / DAY 2

Ascent: 2,880 meters to 3,875 meters
Distance: 8 kilometers
Time: 4 to 5 hours

The trail continues up toward Kibo, passing Second Cave en route, and reaching Third Cave at about 3,875 meters. Most parties spend their second night on the Rongai Route here. Facilities are minimum (toilets only). Water is in the obvious stream below the cave, although you might have to wander downhill a way to find some.

About 20 minutes' walk above (west of) Third Cave, the North Circuit Path leads off to the right (north). There is also a difficult-to-locate trail that leads from Third Cave to Mawenzi Tarn Hut.

From Third Cave, the trail to Kibo Hut is fairly straightforward and traverses up the far northwestern portion of the Saddle between Mawenzi and Kibo. (From Kibo Hut to the summit, see the Kibo section.)

SOUTH CIRCUIT PATH

If you climb any route other than the Marangu Route, you will likely take in some portion of the South Circuit Path. As the name implies, the trail circumnavigates the southern side of Kibo and connects the Shira, Lava Tower, and Barranco Huts, as well as the Barafu and Marangu Routes. The South Circuit Path is extremely well marked and easy to follow.

On its eastern end, the path starts at its intersection with the Marangu Route, near the Saddle. On its western end, the path connects with the Shira Plateau trail as the latter reaches the eastern end of the Shira Plateau, below the Western Breach area.

Because most parties that use the South Circuit Path will travel it from west to east, I have described the trail in this direction.

The South Circuit Trail begins on the Shira Plateau, just east of the North Circuit Path–Shira Plateau trail intersection, east of the red spray paint stating "Moya Hut." The start of the trail is not well marked, and many parties miss it.

From the above intersection, the trail winds down a rocky hill and goes south around Lava Tower, connecting to a junction with the Barranco Hut–Lava Tower Hut trail on a ridge. From this junction, which has several signs and is well marked, it is 2 hours or so of easy hiking down the valley to the east to reach the Barranco Hut area.

The Barranco Hut area is fairly spread out. A camping area lies close to the South Circuit Path; however, the hut itself is located about 10 minutes' walk down the Great Barranco Valley, on the west side of the valley. Two small valleys are crossed to reach the hut from the South Circuit Path.

On the eastern side of the Great Barranco Valley is the Barranco Wall, a 300-meter barrier of volcanic rock that must be negotiated to continue east on the South Circuit Path. From the Barranco Hut area, the path heads north for a few hundred meters, then crosses a river before switchbacking up the wall. Although it's tall and looks incredibly steep, this wall is very easy to climb up or down. It's similar to climbing a set of stairs with the occasional short section of ladder thrown in for good measure. There is very little exposure, and the views are terrific.

The South Circuit Path then crests the Barranco Wall and arrives at a high alpine desert area, best described as a plateau, although it has several small valleys cutting across it from north to south.

The top of the Barranco Wall is the best place to access the southern

Porters near the junction of the South Circuit Path and the Mweka Route, Kilimanjaro (Photo © Cameron M. Burns)

glacier routes (Rebmann, Decken, Kersten, and Heim Glaciers) on Kibo, and a trail leading north toward the glaciers is cairned.

The South Circuit Path then descends and winds its way through the many small valleys crisscrossing the high alpine desert. The last valley on the plateau is the deepest and has a stream running through it, which is the last water for many kilometers. After another few kilometers, the trail meets the Mweka Trail on a ridge. This is the way to access Barafu Huts and Barafu Route. If you are doing the Machame–Mweka combination, turn left (north) and follow this trail.

If you are headed for the Marangu Route, continue east until the Marangu Route is intersected in the Saddle.

If you are going west on the South Circuit Path from the Marangu Route, you may have a hard time finding the start of the trail. It starts in the area of the Saddle, where it is best identified by a small wooden sign saying "Saddle." The South Circuit Path heads east behind this sign.

NORTH CIRCUIT PATH

The North Circuit Path links Third Cave on the Rongai Route to the Shira Plateau trail, between Lava Tower and Shira Hut.

The trail is straightforward to follow, but it takes either a full, hard day of walking, or two fairly easy days to make the circuit from Third Cave to the intersection with the South Circuit Path.

The North Circuit Path crosses numerous rock ribs and gullies on the north side of Kibo but maintains an elevation of around 4,300 meters for most of the circuit. Moir Hut is the only hut on the North Circuit Path, and it is located on the extreme western end of the circuit, near the junction with the Shira Plateau trail. Like most other huts on Kili, it is an unappealing metal shell.

On the east end, the trail can easily be accessed from Kibo Hut, Outward Bound Hut (which lies a few hundred meters north of Kibo Hut), or Third Cave. Small trails that contour around Kibo lead from each of these three places to the North Circuit Path. To access the North Circuit Path from the west (Shira Plateau), see the description for the Shira Plateau Route.

Joined to the South Circuit Path, the North Circuit Trail makes an interesting circumnavigation of Kibo. Most parties take 3 days to do the entire circumnavigation, with stops at Kibo, Moir, and Barranco Huts.

KIBO

There are numerous options to reach the summit of Kibo (5,895 meters/ 19,341 feet), and thus Kilimanjaro, from the high huts on the forest and moorland routes.

Ninety percent of those trying the mountain will opt for the Normal Route, the continuation of the Marangu Route. Probably another 9 percent will opt for either the Barafu Route (from the Barafu Huts to the summit) or the Western Breach Route, a slightly more difficult route that ascends the western side of the mountain, but which has an unwarranted reputation among nontechnical climbers as being very difficult. All three routes require nothing more than lots of warm clothing and a good pair of trekking shoes or boots.

Other major, but rarely climbed, routes on Kibo include the southern glacier routes (Rebmann, Decken, Kersten, and Heim Glaciers) and the Breach Wall area routes.

All the southern glacier and Breach Wall routes have elevation gains of about 1,300 to 1,400 meters; require 5 to 7 kilometers of travel; and take, for the most part, 2 days. The other routes on Kibo (including hiking routes) have elevation gains of about 550 to 1,000 meters; require about 5 kilometers of travel; and take 1 day.

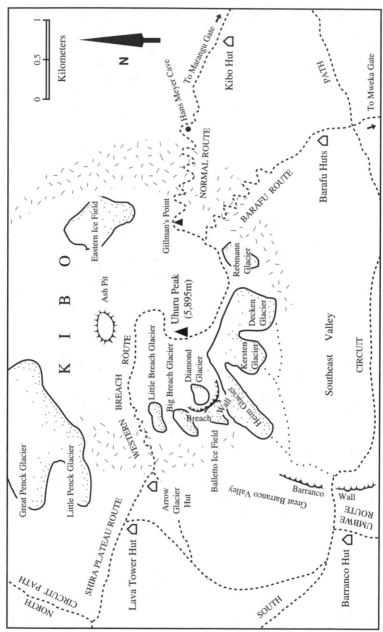

Kibo and the surrounding areas

The following route descriptions begin with the Normal Route (also known as the Marangu Route) and move clockwise around the mountain.

The standard descent for all the technical mountaineering routes on Kibo is to follow one of the walking or scrambling routes (Normal, Barafu, or Western Breach) down.

1. NORMAL ROUTE (WALK)

Although this route has traditionally been called the Normal Route, many people simply call it the Marangu Route, as it's something of an extension of the Marangu forest/moorland route to the summit of Kibo. It was first climbed by M. Lange and Weigele on July 6, 1909.

The trail leaves the Kibo Hut area at 4,700 meters and heads north between the porter/guides buildings, then turns left (west) toward Kibo. Most parties will want to leave the Kibo Hut area at around midnight or 1:00 A.M. to catch sunrise over the summit of Mawenzi, and also because they'll likely be going much more slowly than expected. Also, in the wee hours of the morning, the trail is frozen, so hiking it is not as strenuous as later in the day.

After leaving the buildings, the trail follows fairly gentle terrain up to the Hans Meyer Cave, at about 5,150 meters. Above the cave, the trail steepens considerably as it switchbacks up to Gillman's Point (5,680 meters), on the crater rim.

The attrition rate on the last section of the route to Gillman's Point is tremendous, and it's not uncommon to see dozens of climbers turn back. At Gillman's Point, the summit will come into view across the crater. The trail drops down a few meters into the crater and then follows along the crater rim, passing Stella Point, where the Barafu Route reaches the crater rim and the minor knobs of Hans Meyer Point and Elveda Point.

Although the walk around the crater rim to the summit is not particularly steep anywhere, it is extremely tiring, and it's necessary to rest frequently. It takes about 2 hours for the average person to get from Gillman's Point to Uhuru Peak (5,895 meters/19,341 feet), the highest point on Kilimanjaro.

2. BARAFU ROUTE (WALK)

Like the Marangu Route, the Barafu Route up to the summit is essentially a continuation of a lower route—the Mweka Route—through the forest, and thus it is often referred to as the Mweka Route.

The Barafu Route starts at Barafu Huts (4,600 meters), which sit

The Barafu Route (Route 2) above the Barafu Huts, Kilimanjaro
(Photo © Cameron M. Burns)

atop a prominent ridge on the eastern side of the Southeast Valley. The Southeast Valley lies off to the left as you look at the summit from Barafu Huts. The Barafu Route is steep but does not entail anything harder than a stiff hike.

The route climbs the rocky prow of the rib above the hut before winding its way up a very steep gravel trail to the rim. The trail follows the far right side of the Rebmann Glacier; off to the far right is the Ratzel Glacier, which has melted away so considerably in the last ten years that it's hard to tell it's a glacier.

It takes about 5 to 6 hours to get to Stella Point (5,795 meters), on the rim of the crater, then another hour or so to reach Uhuru Peak (5,895 meters/19,341 feet).

KIBO / SOUTHERN GLACIERS

The southern glaciers lie on the southern side of Kibo and are visible from many places around the mountain. There are three major glaciers (from west to east: the Heim, Kersten, and Decken Glaciers) and one smaller, minor glacier, the Rebmann Glacier, which lies east of the Decken Glacier.

The southern glaciers sit above a large, wide, relatively flat, rocky depression called the Southeast Valley. The Southeast Valley is bounded on the west by the Barranco Wall, and on the east by a rib that runs up Kibo next to the Barafu Route.

The three big glaciers (Heim, Kersten, and Decken) are best approached from the Barranco Hut area (3,900 meters). From the Barranco Hut area, follow the South Circuit Path up the Barranco Wall to the point where the trail crests the Barranco Wall. The Southeast Valley will lie before you to the east.

From the crest, follow a rocky ridge that leads off to the left (north) directly toward the Heim Glacier. There is a line of rock cairns marking the way. The Heim Glacier will be directly ahead; the Kersten and Decken Glaciers will be off to the right (northeast). After 1 kilometer or so, the ridge gives way to the broad gravelly slopes that lie below the glaciers. From this point, the approach to all three glaciers involves hiking across these slopes to the base of each glacier.

The Decken and Kersten glaciers can also be accessed from the east. From the junction of the Marangu or Mweka Routes, follow the South Circuit Path west until you are in the Southeast Valley and the glaciers are visible to the north, then hike straight toward the glacier you intend to climb.

In the eastern side of the Southeast Valley (the Barafu Huts side), there are several areas of low volcanic canyons, just north of the South Circuit Path. These canyons must be negotiated to reach the glaciers. However, they can be crossed in numerous places along the trail and should not create a difficult obstacle.

The Rebmann Glacier is best accessed from the Barafu Huts area (see route description, below).

One important word of caution regarding the southern glacier routes: the glaciers are retreating with time, so they are melting out and their conditions are changing. In general, this means that where icy ramps exist today, steep icefalls could exist five or ten years from the time of this writing. Also, conditions vary greatly from year to year, and from season to season.

Most of the southern glaciers drop off sharply around the rim of Kibo's crater, forming massive seracs. Climbing below these seracs in the late morning and afternoon should be avoided for obvious reasons (they may calve off and crush you).

Most parties hike up to the base of the glaciers and bivouac for the night before starting an ascent.

3. REBMANN GLACIER (GRADE II)

The two-pronged Rebmann Glacier is the easternmost of the southern glacier routes on Kibo and is the easiest of the southern glaciers to climb. Indeed, the crux of the climb is reaching the glacier.

Unlike the other southern glacier routes, the Rebmann Glacier is best accessed from Barafu Huts (4,600 meters); however, getting to the glacier requires dropping down off the rock spur on which the huts sit, and into the Southeast Valley. This can be done near Barafu Huts or partway up the Barafu Route where the rock rib drops down enough to allow you to climb down to the Rebmann Glacier. Care should be taken picking a route off the rock spur. The glacier starts at around 5,200 meters and peters out near the crater rim (5,700 meters), where the Normal Route is joined and followed to Uhuru Peak (5,895 meters). The hardest climbing (Grade II) is at the start of the glacier. The angle lessens as height is gained.

This route takes a half day from Barafu Huts. The first ascent party is unknown.

4. DECKEN GLACIER, RIGHT SIDE (GRADE III–IV)

The right side of the Decken Glacier was first climbed by M. Tudo, J. Montford, F. Shock, and J. Kuhn in August 1974.

The route skirts the difficult rock and ice walls found halfway up the Decken Glacier by traversing right onto an easy ice field that leads to several pitches of steep ice climbing, then tops out at 5,650 meters near the Wedge, a prominent rock fin that separates the Decken and Kersten Glaciers. From the glacier, the Normal Route is followed around the crater rim to Uhuru Peak (5,895 meters).

5. DECKEN GLACIER, ORIGINAL ROUTE (GRADE III–IV)

The Decken Glacier was first climbed by E. Eisenmann and T. Schnackig on January 12, 1938. The first solo ascent was by Ante Mahote in 1964.

This route starts directly below the lower left-hand side of the Decken Glacier, at about 4,650 meters, and follows the line of least resistance up the left-hand side of the glacier. The first half of the route consists of snow climbing up to 65 degrees. Cruxes (Grade III–IV) are encountered where the glacier has melted out to form icefalls. There are several

The Southern Glaciers of Kibo, Kilimanjaro, with Routes 4–10 marked (Photo © Cameron M. Burns)

moderate rock pitches, and rock gear should be carried. About halfway up, at about the 5,200-meter level, the angle of the glacier kicks back dramatically, and the route becomes nothing more than a snow hike, though care should be taken in case of crevasses. Continue north toward Kibo's crater, then join the Normal Route to Uhuru Peak (5,895 meters).

Allow 2 days for an ascent of this route from one of the high huts. There are several rock bivouac sites on the right side of the glacier, about midway up the route.

6. KERSTEN GLACIER, RIGHT SIDE (GRADE V)

First climbed by Mark Savage and Iain Allan in 2 days, July 28–29, 1976, this ascent requires excellent routefinding skills. It starts at about 4,650 meters, below the large rock buttress separating the Kersten and Decken Glaciers, then follows a jumble of seracs and ice steps up and left for many pitches until it gains the prominent ice field below the crest of the glacier. This ice field is very dangerous because of the serac above and afternoon melting.

At the top of the ice field, a gully leads up and left past a series of seracs. Near the top of the gully, move up and right, through a break in the seracs, which leads to easier ground. Above this, the angle lessens, and a steep hike leads to Uhuru Peak (5,895 meters).

7. KERSTEN GLACIER, DIRECT ROUTE (GRADE VI)

This route was first climbed by Ian Howell, Bill O'Connor, and John Cleare on December 20–21, 1975.

Start below the middle of the Kersten Glacier, at about 4,700 meters, and climb straight up a couloir that angles right. At the head of the couloir, climb a steep ice pitch on the left, then the rock wall above to a snow ledge. Move right into a gully and climb steep ice, then traverse farther right, back into the main gully. Climb up the gully to a rock overhang, then skirt it by going left and around it, on snow. Climb straight up for four pitches to a large ice cave at about 5,100 meters, which can be used as a bivouac spot. Move right and climb snow slopes to the crater rim (5,700 meters). The Normal Route is then followed to Uhuru Peak (5,895 meters).

8. KERSTEN GLACIER, ORIGINAL ROUTE (GRADE VI)

This route ascends easy ground on the left side of the glacier, skirting around two steep icefalls and avoiding any serious difficulties. It was first climbed by Walter Welsch and Leo Herncarek on September 20–22, 1962.

Start below the left-hand edge of the glacier (4,700 meters) and climb up to the first icefall. Traverse left up a steep ice slope, then back across right to surmount the icefall. At the second icefall, traverse right, then back left.

Continue through the serac falls at the top of the glacier and cross the summit ice field to the crater rim (5,700 meters). Continue via the Normal Route to Uhuru Peak (5,895 meters).

9. HEIM GLACIER, DIRECT ROUTE (GRADE VI)

This route has one of the hardest ice leads of any of the southern glacier routes up a vertical icicle at 5,200 meters. It was first climbed by Robert Barton and David Morris on December 29–30, 1977.

Separating the Kersten and Heim Glaciers is a huge rock buttress. The toe of the Heim Glacier lies several hundred meters left of the left edge of this buttress, at about 4,650 meters. Climb the snow and ice fields right of the glacier's toe, until below the tall, broad rock wall that houses the seracs of the upper portion of the Heim Glacier. Climb up and right, to an obvious gully with a vertical icicle hanging down it. Climb the 30-meter icicle (Grade VI).

Above the icicle, it is necessary to work around several seracs that bar access to the upper portion of the Heim Glacier. The upper snowfield leads to Uhuru Peak (5,895 meters).

10. HEIM GLACIER (GRADE III)

This is the classic glacier climb on Kilimanjaro, the equivalent of the Polish Glacier on Aconcagua. It was first climbed on September 20–25, 1957, by A. Nelson, H. J. Cooke, and D. N. Goodall over a period of 6 days. The route can be climbed in 1 day, but generally 2 are taken. It is often soloed.

The best place to spend a night before attempting this route is Barranco Hut (3,900 meters) or in a bivouac directly below the glacier itself. From a point at the top of the Barranco Wall on the South Circuit Path at about 4,200 meters, a line of cairns (some missing) marks an indistinct trail that follows a rock rib toward the foot of the glacier. The rock rib peters out, so the last part of the approach lies on gravel and scree.

From the toe of the glacier, climb up and left in a long gully that follows the right side of the Window Buttress, which separates the Heim

Glacier from the Breach Wall area. There are occasional ice steps up the gully, which can be avoided in places by traversing out left on rock, especially in dry years. At the head of the gully is the steepest section of the glacier, which can be traversed around by going either right or left, following the line of least resistance.

Once atop the steepest section of the route, you will find several bivouac sites to the left, on top of the Window Buttress, at about 5,150 meters. From this point, the route ascends the low-angled upper section of the Heim Glacier, staying between the east end of the Breach Wall and ice cliffs on the right side of the upper part of the glacier. There are several bivouac opportunities on this section of the route.

The top of the glacier has retreated from the rim, so the final section of the route is a walk across rubble to the edge of the crater, then on to Uhuru Peak (5,895 meters) via the Normal Route.

KIBO / BREACH WALL

Although the difficult Messner/Renzler Route is often referred to as "the Breach Wall," there are, in fact, several routes up the Breach Wall, the Messner/Renzler Route being the most notorious and direct.

The Breach Wall is a massive block of stone that protrudes from the southwestern edge of Kibo. It contains two glaciers on its slopes— the Balletto Ice Field, which is halfway up the wall, and the Diamond Glacier, which sits atop the Breach Wall and provides moisture for the famous Breach Wall Icicle. Ironically, the three routes that climb portions of the wall are, for the most part, snow-and-ice routes.

The Breach Wall is best accessed from the Barranco Hut area (3,900 meters), which lies just down the Great Barranco Valley from the wall. To reach the Breach Wall, hike up the South Circuit Path, as if you are heading for Lava Tower, for about 1 kilometer. When the Breach Wall is visible off to the right, hike toward it. There are several small drainages that must be crossed before the base of the wall is reached, but which pose little problem. Crampons can be helpful for this approach.

11. BREACH WALL, EAST END (GRADE V+)

The first ascent of this route was made by John Temple and Anthony Charlton on December 22–23, 1974.

The Breach Wall area, Kilimanjaro, with Routes 10, 12, and 14–16 marked (Photo © Cameron M. Burns)

At the base of the Breach Wall (4,600 meters), is a huge, cascading icefall that leads from the talus slopes at the foot of the wall to the Balletto Ice Field. Climb the icefall to the ice field, then climb up and right to the foot of the upper wall (5,450 meters), where it is possible to bivouac.

Move right along the foot of the upper wall to the left-hand edge of the Heim Glacier. Follow the Heim Glacier, or the scree slopes to its left, to Uhuru Peak (5,895 meters).

12. BREACH WALL, DIRECT ROUTE (GRADE VI)

The first ascent of this difficult climb was made by Reinhold Messner and Konrad Renzler on January 31, 1978.

At the base of the Breach Wall (4,600 meters) is a huge, cascading icefall that leads from the talus slopes at the foot of the wall to the Balletto Ice Field. Climb the icefall to the ice field, then carefully climb the ice field up and left to the Breach Wall Icicle (5,450 meters). Climb the 90-meter icicle to the Diamond Glacier and continue north to Uhuru Peak (5,895 meters).

It is possible to bivouac behind the Icicle itself, or down to the right of the Balletto Ice Field (5,400 meters), near the Window Buttress.

There is much rockfall on this route, especially on the lower half. Anyone contemplating an ascent would do well to spend a couple of nights at Barranco Hut, studying the route. On the trail between Barranco Hut and Lava Tower, you can hear rockfall crashing down the wall throughout the day.

13. BREACH WALL, BALLETTO ICE FIELD (GRADE VI)

First ascent by John Temple and Dave Cheesmond on April 1–4, 1975.

This route climbs the rock wall to the left of the icefall that constitutes the start of the Breach Wall Direct Route. From 4,700 meters, six pitches up the rock wall (using aid in places) lead to a notch looking down over the icefall. From here, work up onto the ice field itself and climb to the base of the upper wall that houses the Direct Route's Icicle. Traverse right along the base of the wall to a gully. Climb the gully on a mixture of rock and ice pitches to easier ground near Uhuru Peak (5,895 meters). There are several bivouac sites on this route, at the base of the upper wall and near the base of the gully.

14. LORTSCHER ROUTE (GRADE V)

This route was first ascended by Fritz Lortscher, solo, on January 11–12, 1972. Beginning at 4,700 meters, skirt the lower left-hand edge of the Breach Wall, following broken ledges and easy ground to the western edge of the Diamond Glacier. Then continue north to Uhuru Peak (5,895 meters).

15. BREACH GLACIERS ROUTE (GRADE III)

The route was first climbed by Fritz Lortscher and J. Mayer on January 10, 1972.

A straightforward and direct route, the Breach Glaciers Route climbs the huge gully left (west) of the Breach Wall, beginning at about 4,700 meters and following the gully all the way to its top, near Uhuru Peak. It may be necessary to exit the top of the gully to the right, which puts one on the Diamond Glacier, depending on conditions. From the top of the gully (and the Diamond Glacier), Uhuru Peak (5,895 meters) will be a short hike to the east.

16. WESTERN BREACH ROUTE (SCRAMBLE)

Also known as the Arrow Glacier Route and the Great Western Arch, this excellent route is a classic scramble. It does not actually climb the Arrow Glacier, but scree and easy rock up and left of the glacier.

The route is exposed, but the climbing is no harder than a scramble (American Class 3). Trekkers will likely feel a little bit out of place on this route; technical mountaineers will run right up it. Crampons are not necessary; however, they make the descent easier.

The route starts at ruinous Arrow Glacier Hut (which is the best place to camp the night before an ascent), at 4,900 meters. At the Arrow Glacier, examine the huge amphitheater above. It runs from the western end of the massive Breach Wall around to a major, but broken rock buttress on the left end (which might not be visible from the hut itself.) Halfway across this huge amphitheater, and almost directly above Arrow Glacier Hut, is a low-angled minor rock rib that runs vertically up into the amphitheater wall.

Climb the small talus and scree hill above Arrow Glacier Hut, then follow the left-hand edge of the rock rib for about 600 meters until the foot of the amphitheater wall is reached and the rib steepens. At this point, it is necessary to move right, onto the rib itself, and to follow the well-worn trail as it negotiates the steepest section of the route. The climbing is only scrambling, but it is somewhat exposed in places. The rib ends at the crater rim, at 5,500 meters, where the trail flattens out and skirts right of a summit ice field along the edge of the Western Breach. After 20 minutes of walking, the final hill leading to

The final hill leading to the summit, Western Breach Route (Route 16), Kilimanjaro (Photo © Cameron M. Burns)

Uhuru Peak (5,895 meters) will be obvious off to the left. The trail ascends the easy ground left of the prominent buttress via a series of strenuous switchbacks. At the top of the switchbacks, the summit is an easy half hour's walk away, to the northeast. Be sure to keep an eye on landmarks as you approach the summit, as getting back to the top of the switchbacks can be confusing.

KIBO / NORTHWESTERN GLACIERS

The northwestern glaciers on Kibo are rarely visited, simply because they lie so far from any trailheads and most trails on the mountain.

Perhaps the most significant thing about the northwestern glaciers is that they have retreated so much since they were originally named and mapped that they bear very little resemblance to their original selves.

Western Breach Route (Route 16), Kilimanjaro
(Photo © Cameron M. Burns)

Indeed, maps of these glaciers from the 1960s show them all connected, a situation that is far from true today.

The northwestern glaciers are best accessed from the North Circuit Path, which can be reached from most of the other trails on Kilimanjaro.

17. LITTLE PENCK GLACIER (GRADE III)

This two-pronged glacier lying immediately west of the massive Western Breach area was first climbed on June 20, 1969, by D. Payne and D. King. The route taken by the first ascent party started at the foot of the Great Penck Glacier (4,900 meters) and traversed rock and ice cliffs up and right to reach the snout of the left prong of the Little Penck Glacier. The remainder of the glacier offers a steep (50 to 60 degrees) hike up to the crater rim at about 5,700 meters. Once on the rim, walk southeast, along the top of the Western Breach area, to Uhuru Peak (5,895 meters).

The right-hand side of the glacier (Grade III) has also been climbed.

18. GREAT PENCK GLACIER (GRADE II)

This glacier has retreated considerably in recent times. It is the obvious tongue of ice left from the Little Penck Glacier and offers a steep hike from about 4,900 meters. It was first climbed by J. Pike and P. A. Campbell on September 14, 1960. The upper part of the glacier has melted away, so it requires scrambling on scree up to the crater rim, which is reached at about 5,700 meters. Once on the crater rim, hike southeast, passing along the top of the Western Breach area, to Uhuru Peak (5,895 meters).

19. CREDNER GLACIER (GRADE II)

Along the North Circuit Trail about 1 kilometer past the Great Penck Glacier is the Credner Glacier. This long glacier offers an easy hike from 4,900 meters to the crater rim (5,700 meters) on Kibo. Once on the rim, walk southeast, along the top of the Western Breach area, to Uhuru Peak (5,895 meters).

The first ascent party is unknown.

Kibo from the Shira Plateau, Kilimanjaro, with Routes 12 and 16–19 marked (Photo © Cameron M. Burns)

MAWENZI

Mawenzi is rarely climbed: because there are no trekking routes up the mountain, it probably receives only one or two ascents a year. All the routes on Mawenzi require technical rock climbing (ropes, hardware, and so forth), which is usually mixed in with a little ice climbing, depending on the conditions.

The other feature that distinguishes Mawenzi from its big sister Kibo is that Mawenzi is a complex mass of summits, most of which are difficult to reach from one another. It is basically a north-south rock ridge, with spurs of rock running off from the main ridge. The highest summit is Hans Meyer Peak (5,149 meters/16,893 feet), named after the geographer who made the first ascent of Kibo.

Although it is overlooked by most climbers, Mawenzi is the third-highest summit on the African continent after Kibo and Mount Kenya.

Only the two most frequently climbed routes on Hans Meyer Peak—Oehler Gully and the Northwest Ridge—are described here.

There are two bases from which an ascent of Mawenzi can be easily made: Mawenzi Hut (4,600 meters), on the western side of the peak, and Mawenzi Tarn Hut (4,300 meters), on the north side of the peak. Both huts are small and very primitive. Both are reached by hiking north on the obvious marked trail from Horombo Hut on the Marangu Route. From Horombo Hut (3,700 meters) to Mawenzi Hut, it is a 2- to 3-hour hike. To reach Mawenzi Tarn Hut, continue north on the trail from Mawenzi Hut, passing several buttresses and crossing Mawenzi's Northwest Ridge to reach Mawenzi Tarn, and the hut. Water is available at both huts.

Mawenzi Tarn Hut can also be reached from the area of Third Cave on the Rongai Route; however, this trail is rarely used and not well marked.

Descents on Mawenzi are via the route of ascent.

20. HANS MEYER PEAK / NORDECKE PEAK, OEHLER GULLY ROUTE (GRADE IV)

The standard route on Hans Meyer Peak, the tallest point on Mawenzi, is the Oehler Gully. This prominent gully leads to a notch in the ridge between Nordecke Peak (to the north) and the summit of Hans Meyer Peak (to the south). It was first climbed by Edward Oehler and Fritz Klute on July 29, 1912.

Mawenzi from the Saddle, Kilimanjaro, with Routes 20 and 21 marked (Photo © Cameron M. Burns)

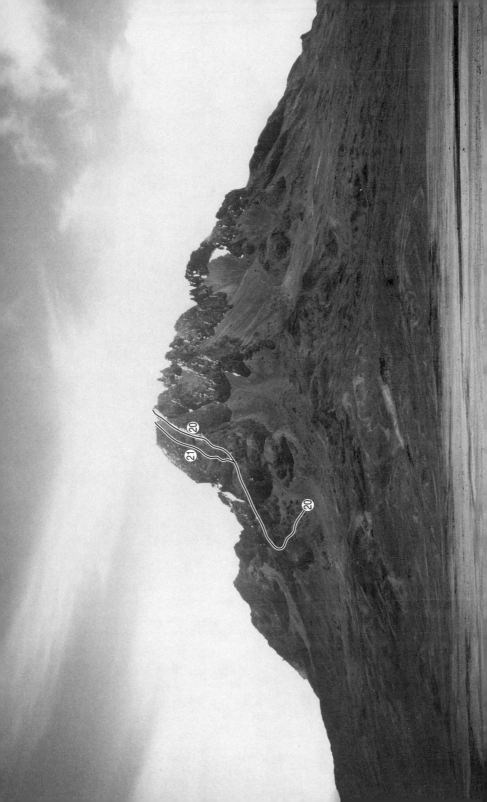

From Mawenzi Hut (4,600 meters), traverse north (left) along the scree field below the west face to the massive West Buttress. Climb up and right, into the col above the West Buttress, then traverse along the top of the ridge to a rock wall called the Big Step. Skirt the Big Step to the right and enter the Oehler Gully. Climb the gully for several pitches to the notch between Nordecke (to the left, or north) and Hans Meyer Peak (to the right, or south). Scramble up to the summit (5,149 meters). The difficulty of the gully depends on conditions. Generally, with more ice and snow, it is easier.

Descent is made via the gully, although it is common to climb out of the gully onto the walls to each side if rockfall is hazardous.

21. HANS MEYER PEAK / NORDECKE PEAK, NORTHWEST RIDGE ROUTE (GRADE II)

The first ascent of this route was by R. F. Davies, solo, in January 1953.

From Mawenzi Hut (4,600 meters), climb the Oehler Gully Route past the Big Step to a point 25 meters left of the Oehler Gully, then climb up a gully following a dike that leads to the Northwest Ridge proper. Follow the ridge all the way to the summit of Nordecke (5,140 meters/16,863 feet), then traverse across the notch at the top of the Oehler Gully to Hans Meyer Peak (5,149 meters).

CHAPTER 5

MOUNT KENYA

*We passed the night without disturbance, and rose with the
sun. Kenya peak glittered superbly in the sky...*
— Halford John Mackinder in his diary,
August 26, 1899

Mount Kenya is a mountaineers' mountain.

Steep, craggy, and with twin summit spires, it's the kind of peak
mountaineers might conjure up when they dream of serious climbing
adventures. It resembles some of the legendary peaks of Patagonia, the
Matterhorn, and certain mountains in the Canadian Rockies.

At 5,199 meters (17,058 feet), Mount Kenya is also the second-
highest mountain in Africa after Kilimanjaro.

Mount Kenya is much more intriguing to mountaineers than
Kilimanjaro. For one thing, it took until nearly the end of the last
century for explorers to even confirm the existence of the mysterious
peak. Felice Benuzzi's famed 1953 story of three Italian prisoners of
war escaping from a British prison camp near Nanyuki so they could
climb the mountain, then their "escape" back into prison after bagging
Point Lenana, adds to the allure (see Appendix C, Further Reading).

Besides the historical intrigue, Mount Kenya lies just 17 kilometers
north of the equator, is 500 meters lower than Kili, and yet it boasts the
best ice climbs in Africa, and some of the finest in the world.

Like most other mountains in East Africa, Mount Kenya is an
extinct volcano, which last erupted 3.5 million years ago. The volcanic uplift created an island ecosystem, known today as the Central
Highlands. Mount Kenya is at the center of these highlands.

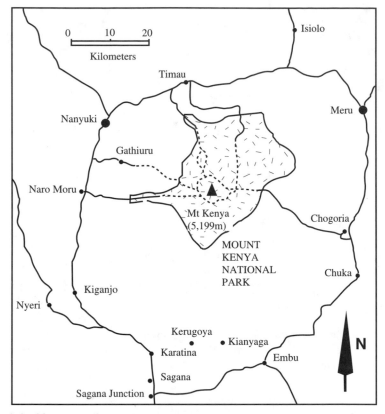

Mt. Kenya and vicinity

The Mount Kenya massif is circular in shape, about 70 kilometers in diameter, and rises about 5,000 meters from the 800-meter surrounding plains.

Like Kilimanjaro, Mount Kenya boasts several distinct zones of flora and fauna: the cultivated slopes around the national park boundaries, the bamboo forests, the high moorlands around the main peaks, and finally the alpine desert zone, which is mostly rock and ice.

Mount Kenya National Park was created in 1949 and was recently declared an international biosphere reserve by the United Nations Educational, Scientific, and Cultural Organization (UNESCO). The park covers 715 square kilometers and takes in most of the land area above 3,200 meters.

Mount Kenya encompasses more than just one peak. It contains

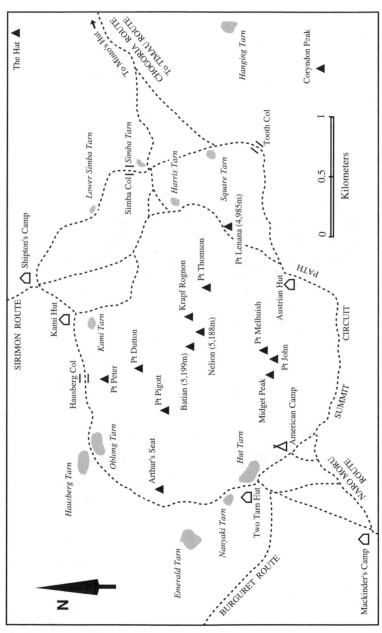

Overview of Mount Kenya

multiple rock spires and summits, a handful of glaciers, and numerous pristine valleys. The three highest peaks are Batian (5,199 meters/17,058 feet), Nelion (5,188 meters/17,021 feet), and Point Lenana (4,985 meters/16,355 feet).

The big difference between Mount Kenya and Kilimanjaro is that the summits of Batian and Nelion cannot be reached by trekkers; they require technical mountaineering skills and equipment.

Point Lenana can be climbed by trekkers without any special mountaineering skills or equipment. Often when trekkers say they have climbed Mount Kenya, they are really referring to an ascent of Lenana.

THE NAME

To the indigenous people who lived in central Kenya for thousands of years, Mount Kenya had various names.

The Kikuyu, who make up the bulk of Kenya's modern-day population, called the mountain Kirinyaga, which, roughly translated, means "white or bright mountain." They believed the mountain to be the home of their great god Ngai, and out of respect, many still build their houses so that the doors face Mount Kenya.

The Embu called the mountain Kirenia ("mountain of whiteness"), and the Masai called it Oldonyo Eibor ("white mountain") and Oldonyo Egere ("speckled mountain").

Anthropologists and linguists believe the modern name *Kenya* comes from the Kamba or Wakamba tribe, who called the mountain Kiinyaa ("mountain of the ostrich") because the dark rock and speckled ice fields closely resemble the tail feathers of the male ostrich.

The three highest points on Mount Kenya—Batian, Nelion, and Point Lenana—were all named by Halford Mackinder after legendary Masai *laibons*, or medicine men, following the first ascent of the mountain. The Masai who live around Mount Kenya believed that their divine ancestors lived on Mount Kenya and that their people came down from the mountain at the beginning of time.

Most of the other subsidiary summits around Mount Kenya are named for more contemporary European explorers and climbers.

POPULARITY

According to Mount Kenya National Park estimates, about 16,000 people visit the park annually. Of those, most climb Point Lenana, and probably 60 percent make its summit.

About 500 each year attempt to climb the Normal Route on Nelion, and about 200 of these reach its summit. Surprisingly to most serious mountaineers, only an estimated 50 climbers reach the summit of Batian each year, most by following the Normal Route to Nelion, then traversing across the Gate of the Mists.

One of the best things about climbing Batian or Nelion is that if you have a few days to wait, you can pick a day when you will have the mountain all to yourself!

GEOGRAPHY

There are five "approach" routes (Naro Moru, Chogoria, Sirimon, Burguret, and Timau) that penetrate the forest and moorland areas on Mount Kenya. These routes, which can all be done by trekkers, do not go to the summit of any peak, not even Point Lenana. They all end at the Summit Circuit Path, which circumnavigates the main peaks of Mount Kenya.

From the Summit Circuit Path there are dozens of options open to you, from hiking up to Point Lenana from Austrian Hut or Shipton's Camp, to climbing Batian and Nelion. If you are doing a trek or climb with an outfitter or guide, you must decide which route or routes you want to take to any of Mount Kenya's various summits (if any) with your outfitter before you leave Naro Moru, Chogoria, Nanyuki, Nairobi, or wherever.

FOREST / MOORLAND ROUTES

The three main forest and moorland routes leading to the main peaks of Mount Kenya are the Naro Moru, Chogoria, and Sirimon Routes. These routes are well established and well marked, and offer easy-to-follow trails into the high country. The other two approach routes, the Burguret and Timau Routes, are not well established, and even getting to their trailheads is an experiment in exploration. Regardless of how good your map-reading and navigational skills are, you will invariably get lost at some point on either of the two routes.

Perhaps the most important thing to remember about the Naro Moru, Chogoria, and Sirimon Routes is that they have national park gates, and you can pay your park fees upon entrance or exit from the park. If you use the Burguret or Timau Routes, however, you must make sure that either you, or a hired outfitter, pays the fees at the Naro Moru Gate.

Many climbers will want to combine two of the forest and moorland routes to make a complete traverse of the mountain. There are numerous options, obviously, but probably the prettiest traverse is the Chogoria–Sirimon traverse.

All of the trailheads are accessed from the tarmac ring road that circles Mount Kenya National Park. From the south (Nairobi), this unnamed ring road starts at Sagana Junction, a small village strung along the highway. The main Nairobi–Nanyuki Road becomes the western half of the ring road at Sagana Junction; the eastern half of the ring road is a subsidiary road at this point.

To quickly reach Chogoria, Meru, and other points around the eastern half of the mountain, turn right at Sagana Junction. To reach Naro Moru, Nanyuki, Timau, and other villages on the northern and western side of the mountain, go straight at Sagana Junction.

The following routes are described in order of popularity. Each route description is broken down into days, the way a typical party would ascend the mountain to the Summit Circuit Path.

NARO MORU ROUTE

The Naro Moru Route is the most popular way to the higher elevations on Mount Kenya. It ascends the mountain's forest and moorland areas from the west. The route is not particularly scenic but is generally the one chosen by most tour and outfitting companies because of its fancy tourist accommodations.

Naro Moru itself is little more than a collection of shacks and shops strung out along the road. It lies about 200 kilometers north of Nairobi, and about 60 kilometers north of Sagana Junction.

The road to the park gate is well marked. Officially, it is Route D448, and a big sign announces that it is 12 kilometers to Munyu (a tiny village en route to the Naro Moru Gate).

Just west of the main Naro Moru intersection, where the ring road meets Route D448, is the popular but expensive Naro Moru River Lodge. Porters and guides can be arranged here, along with transport to and from trailheads. Also, just 7.2 kilometers north of the Naro Moru intersection is the Mountain Rock Lodge. It is similar to the Naro Moru River Lodge, and guides and porters can be arranged here as well.

From the Naro Moru intersection, drive east on the dirt road for 13.8 kilometers to a split in the road. Take the right road, and drive another 2.2 kilometers to another split. Take the left branch. An office of the National Outdoor Leadership School (NOLS) will be on the left, 1.8 kilometers up this road; 0.7 kilometer beyond NOLS is the Youth Hostel Camp; 2.7 kilometers beyond the Youth Hostel Camp, the road splits again. Go left. Another 4.7 kilometers leads to the Naro Moru Gate and the Mount Kenya National Park headquarters (2,500 meters).

Most climbers begin hiking at the park gate, although it is possible to drive a vehicle as far as the Met Station (3,050 meters).

NARO MORU ROUTE: NARO MORU GATE TO MET STATION / DAY 1

Ascent: 2,500 meters to 3,050 meters
Distance: 10 kilometers
Time: 3 to 4 hours

From the Naro Moru Gate, the trail leads through the forest along a ridge between the two branches of the Naro Moru River. About 6 to 7 kilometers from the park gate, the trail crosses Percival's Bridge, then continues north, then east again, as it gains the upper Teleki Valley. The trail soon reaches the Meteorological Station ("Met Station") at 3,050 meters. The Met Station has several bunkhouses as well as camping sites. Most parties spend their first night on the Naro Moru Route here.

NARO MORU ROUTE: MET STATION TO MACKINDER'S CAMP / DAY 2

Ascent: 3,050 meters to 4,200 meters
Distance: 10 kilometers
Time: 5 hours

The normal second day's hiking continues east, up the trail, passing a radio tower and emerging from the forest at about 3,200 meters. The steepest, wettest portion of the moorland is called the Vertical Bog, for obvious reasons. Just picture yourself here in the rainy season! Continuing east, the trail splits: the left branch follows the Naro Moru River; the more popular right branch follows a ridge to the south and joins the river higher up. After a full 5 hours, Mackinder's Camp (4,200 meters) is reached.

Mackinder's Camp has a large bunkhouse, as well as many possible campsites. Most parties spend their second night on the mountain here.

From Mackinder's Camp, the trail continues up the Teleki Valley, moving right toward the top of the valley, where it joins the Summit

Circuit Path. At the Summit Circuit Path, you have the option of going north around the west side of the mountain, to American Camp and Two Tarn Hut, or continuing east around the south side of the mountain to Austrian Hut and the Lewis Glacier area.

If you are trekking, your third day will most likely be a hike up to Point Lenana, then an afternoon return to the Met Station for one night before hiking out to Naro Moru. Most climbers at Mackinder's Camp who are headed to Point Lenana get up extremely early so they can catch the sunrise over the mountain. It takes about 4 to 5 hours to reach Point Lenana from Mackinder's Camp, and the elevation gain is about 800 meters. The trail to Lenana—which goes east, around the south side of the main peaks—is extremely steep and on loose gravel, so it is important to go slowly.

If you are doing technical mountaineering, your third day will most likely be a matter of getting to one of the huts below your proposed route and setting up camp for the night.

SIRIMON ROUTE

After the Chogoria Route, the Sirimon Route is probably the second most scenic route accessing the upper portions of Mount Kenya.

To reach the Sirimon Route, drive 15.8 kilometers east from Nanyuki on the Mount Kenya ring road to a dirt road leading to the Sirimon Gate. From the village of Timau, drive 6 kilometers west to the dirt road (or 56 kilometers west from Meru). The road to the Sirimon Gate is well marked with a huge wooden sign.

It's a short 1.1-kilometer drive to the forest gate, then 8 kilometers more to the national park gate. There are several splits in the road before the park gate: stay left at each one.

SIRIMON ROUTE: SIRIMON GATE TO JUDMAIER CAMP / OLD MOSES / DAY 1

Ascent: 2,700 meters to 3,300 meters
Distance: 9 kilometers
Time: 3 to 4 hours

It is 9 kilometers from the Sirimon Gate through the forest to the Judmaier Camp/Old Moses area (3,300 meters). Most people choose to drive this section of the road, but some walk it to aid acclimatization. The road is obvious and well maintained.

Most parties spend their first night on the Sirimon Route at Judmaier

Camp, a cleared camping area on the left side of the road, or at the Old Moses bunkhouse, another few hundred yards farther down the road.

SIRIMON ROUTE: JUDMAIER CAMP / OLD MOSES TO SHIPTON'S CAMP / DAY 2

Ascent: 3,300 meters to 4,200 meters
Distance: 12 kilometers
Time: 5 to 6 hours

From Old Moses, the main summits of Batian, Nelion, and Point Lenana are visible, as are the subsidiary peaks of Terere and Sendeyo, to the left of the main peaks.

From the Judmaier Camp/Old Moses area, there are two alternative trails to Shipton's Camp: the first via the Mackinder Valley, the second via Liki North Hut. Most parties follow the Mackinder Valley Route, as the trail is much easier to follow. Some porters will not follow the Liki North Hut alternative and must be met at Shipton's Camp if you use this route. A map and compass are helpful.

The main trail, via the Mackinder Valley, follows a rough four-wheel-drive road and continues south (keep right, as other roads lead off left) before petering out as it circles around a creekbed, the Ontulili River. A hundred meters beyond the creek, the trail leaves the old roadbed, going west (left). It is not well marked but should be obvious. The trail contours along the northern slopes of the massif for about 4 kilometers, gradually turning south and cresting an insignificant ridge. Descend the next valley, cross the Liki North River, then climb out of the valley to the south. The trail crests another ridge, this one above the spectacular Mackinder Valley.

The trail descends into the Mackinder Valley and follows the eastern side of the valley for about 7 kilometers to Shipton's Camp (4,200 meters).

The Liki North Hut variation starts up the same rough four-wheel-drive road. After passing three subsidiary roads on the left, follow the fourth to its end. The fourth road is about an hour from Judmaier Camp. The trail continues from this point, heading toward the Barrow, a rounded hill to the south. It skirts right of the Barrow, along the northwest side of the hill, the crosses the heads of the Ontulili and Liki north Valleys before reaching Liki North Hut (4,000 meters). The small hut doesn't offer much shelter, but there are plenty of campsites around it. From Liki North Hut, the trail climbs out of the Liki North Valley, crests a ridge, then descends into the Mackinder Valley, where it joins the Mackinder Valley Route.

It's a straightforward walk up the valley to Shipton's Camp, where there are a bunkhouse and several camping areas. Most parties spend their second night on the Sirimon Route here.

From Shipton's Camp, you have several options. You can continue up the main trail south, which climbs to Simba Col, then joins the Chogoria Route near Square Tarn. Or you can hike up the hill to the right, which leads to Kami Hut, below the north face of Batian. In between these two options is a trail that climbs Point Lenana. It leads up (south-southeast) through a narrow gully, then switchbacks up a steep gravel hill before reaching Harris Tarn. The trail goes around the north side of Harris Tarn, then scrambles up the northeast side of Point Lenana.

CHOGORIA ROUTE

The Chogoria Route is by far the most scenic and interesting route through the forests and moorland areas of Mount Kenya National Park. It is reached from the Chogoria Village area, on the east side of the park.

To reach Chogoria, drive north from Nairobi and turn right at Sagana Junction. Follow this road for many kilometers, through the towns of Embu and Chuka. About 16 kilometers past Chuka is a turnoff on the left. Look for signs pointing to the Transit Motel. The Transit Motel, located about 2 kilometers up this road, is an excellent place to stay, with very reasonable rates and a superfriendly staff. Chogoria Village is about 2 kilometers north of the Transit Motel turnoff on the Mount Kenya ring road, then up a dirt road to the east.

Guides, porters, and lifts to the park gate can be arranged at the Transit Motel. (Ask to see Lawrence Gitonga of the Chogoria Porters and Guides Association. He'll set you up with whatever you need. Tell him Cam sent you.) The entire village of Chogoria is in the Mount Kenya guiding/portering business, and everyone here is related. Apparently a couple of generations ago, Chogoria chief Mbogori Mwenda had thirty-seven wives and greatly contributed to the town's population.

From the Transit Motel, the road continues west. After about 2 kilometers, turn left, and drive past Mutindwa Market and Village. The road will circle around to the south, then reach a turnoff to the right leading to the Mount Kenya forest gate and the national park. There is a Kenya Ministry of Environment and Natural Resources green-and-white sign where you should turn right; it will be obvious.

A few kilometers up the road is the forest gate. You will need to sign in at the gate register, using your passport number.

CHOGORIA ROUTE: FOREST GATE TO MERU MOUNT KENYA LODGE (CHOGORIA PARK GATE) / DAY 1

Ascent: 1,700 meters to 3,000 meters
Distance: 23 kilometers
Time: 10 to 11 hours

Although many groups walk from Chogoria Village to the forest gate on their first day, and from the forest gate to Meru Mount Kenya Lodge on the second day, most parties get a lift at least to the forest gate.

From the forest gate, it's about 23 kilometers up the dirt road to the park gate. This section of road passes through some wild forests, and it is not uncommon to encounter elephant and buffalo here.

Just before the park boundary, off to the right, is the Meru Mount Kenya Lodge—actually a collection of cabins (more commonly known as the *banda*s) built around a grassy common. They offer hot showers, kitchen, bedroom, and small lounge and cost about US$25 per night per person. Most parties climbing the Chogoria Route stay here their first night, and if you are slow at acclimatizing, it might be wise to spend two nights here. The *banda*s are located just outside the national park boundaries, so you don't have to pay the park entrance fee until you actually enter the park.

CHOGORIA ROUTE: MERU MOUNT KENYA LODGE (CHOGORIA PARK GATE) TO MINTO'S HUT / DAY 2

Ascent: 3,000 meters to 4,300 meters
Distance: 15 kilometers
Time: 6 to 7 hours

From the bandas, you will need to walk through the park gate and pay entrance fees. Then it's an easy 7-kilometer stroll up the four-wheel-drive road to the roadhead. You can drive as far as the roadhead, which is the only one on Mount Kenya where tourists regularly leave vehicles.

Near the roadhead is an interesting side trip that many climbers may want to take. Just south of the roadhead is a stream that leads to a beautiful waterfall. A trail on the south side of the stream follows it for about 0.5 kilometer to the top of the falls. A small, very steep trail goes down the west (right) side of the falls to the bottom. Also, just west of the falls is an amphitheater containing a cave used by the Mau Mau rebels in the early 1950s. The cave—filled with goat dung—was bombed by the British; some guides might not want to take you here for fear of there still being live shells in the area.

From the roadhead, the Chogoria trail crosses the creek to the south, then climbs a long east-west ridge for several kilometers. The trail eventually crests a ridge that overlooks the spectacular Gorges Valley. The trail then follows the north (right) side of the gorge for several more kilometers to Hall Tarns and Minto's Hut, the normal second night's stay on the Chogoria Route. Minto's Hut is small, basic, and pretty filthy. There are many campsites around it.

CHOGORIA ROUTE: MINTO'S HUT TO AUSTRIAN HUT / DAY 3

Ascent: 4,300 meters to 4,800 meters
Distance: 10 kilometers
Time: 5 to 6 hours

From Minto's Hut, most parties continue on to Austrian Hut, although there are other options.

From Minto's, the trail continues west to a large flat area known as Temple Fields, where it meets the Summit Circuit Path. At this point, there are two options. In the first, you can hike southwest (following the left branch of the trail) to reach Tooth Col and Austrian Hut. This route climbs a steep scree field before crossing Tooth Col between several rock towers. In the second option, the right branch of the trail (which heads north) goes to Simba Col and then drops down a long hill to Shipton's Camp.

Most trekking groups take the first option to Austrian Hut, where they spend a third night before climbing Point Lenana the next morning. Technical mountaineers headed for the Normal Route on Batian/ Nelion also usually go to Austrian Hut.

BURGURET ROUTE

The Burguret Route should not be considered a trail, track, or path like the other routes on the mountain. It is a "route" only in the sense that it is one way you can go. Put another way, the Burguret Route is little more than a narrow track through the woods on its most pronounced sections. On its least pronounced sections, the trail is nonexistent.

The route begins near the little settlement of Gathiuru (1,500 meters), southeast of Nanyuki. There is no official trailhead for this route, and getting on the route is a matter of trial and error.

To reach Gathiuru from Nanyuki, drive southwest on the Mount Kenya ring road for 8.5 kilometers. To reach Gathiuru from Naro Moru, drive northeast on the Mount Kenya ring road for 7.2 kilometers. The road to Gathiuru is well signed. Officially, it is called Route E642. There is also a green-and-white sign pointing to "Ministry of Environment and Natural Resources, Forest Department's Gathiuru Forest Station."

Follow this dirt road southeast for 11.1 kilometers to the forest gate. Immediately after the forest gate, turn sharp right. The road immediately splits; take the left branch. The road will pass a small village on the left that looks like an early American pilgrim settlement. Then, 0.4 kilometer past the gate, the main road veers right while a small, very rough road continues straight toward the mountain. Take the rough road straight for 2.3 kilometers, then turn right into a forest.

The forest is only about 0.5 kilometer wide, and the road soon re-emerges into cultivated fields. However, about halfway though the forest, an old, impassable road leads off right. This is the start of the Burguret Route. There are no signs, no facilities. Nothing. (To get an idea of where the Burguret Route goes, continue driving through the forest to the fields on the east side. From this cleared agricultural area, you can look up at the lower slopes of the mountain. A small, rounded hill is where the route goes.)

The Burguret Route is almost the same route taken by Felice Benuzzi and his compatriots when they escaped from a POW camp in 1943 (see Appendix C, Further Reading).

Two guides who know the route well are Leonard Josphat and Ambrose Kirimi in Chogoria. They are highly recommended and can be contacted through the Chogoria Porters and Guides Association, P.O. Box 114, Chogoria, Tharaka-Nithi, Kenya.

BURGURET ROUTE: ROAD END TO KAMPI YA MACHENGENI / DAY 1

Ascent: 2,000 meters to 3,000 meters
Distance: 9 kilometers
Time: 7 to 8 hours

Although extremely difficult to follow at times, the route ascends an indistinct ridge between the Burguret and Nanyuki Rivers. Much of the walking requires bushwhacking through bamboo forests, and inevitably everyone gets lost. The trail emerges at a sloping clearing between the bamboo forests and the heather forests above, called Kampi Ya Machengeni.

Burguret Route: Kampi Ya Machengeni to Highland Castle / Day 2

> **Ascent:** 3,000 meters to 3,700 meters
> **Distance:** 7 kilometers
> **Time:** 7 hours

As the bamboo forest gives way to heather, the trail does not become any more pronounced, except that much of the route is marked with ancient wooden elevation signs. Some of these signs are so old and worn they are easily missed.

The route emerges from the heather (3,500 meters) and continues up the upper Burguret River drainage. Eventually, Highland Castle (3,700 meters)—a long, low rock wall on the left side of the valley—is reached. Most parties spend their second night at Highland Castle.

Burguret Route: Highland Castle to Two Tarn Hut / Day 3

> **Ascent:** 3,700 meters to 4,500 meters
> **Distance:** 9 kilometers
> **Time:** 7 hours

From Highland Castle, the route follows the ridge above Highland Castle and aims straight for the main peaks. After a half day's walk, one reaches Two Tarn Hut, on the west side of the mountain. The Summit Circuit Path is joined, and any portion of the mountain can be reached from this.

Timau Route

This route is rarely used, and is not recommended because of the horrendously long, rough, dirt road approach, which takes you all over the northern side of the mountain, through endless farm country and numerous villages. Also, the trail is not well established, and in some places, is nonexistent. A map and compass are required for this route.

Like the Burguret Route, the Timau Route is a wilderness experience.

To get to the trailhead, drive west on the Mount Kenya ring road from Meru for about 43 kilometers, or east from Nanyuki for 21.8 kilometers to a dirt road that leads south. At the intersection, there are several distinguishing signs, one announcing "District Officer Timau," another "Siraji Limited Homegrown."

Take this dirt road, which crosses a streambed, then enters the Ngusisi Market, a commercial area of shops. Take the left fork of the road and drive straight through the market. Beyond the market the road curves right, over a very rough bridge, then climbs a small hill and meets an intersection 2.4 kilometers from the tarmac road. Turn left, and pass a huge house on the left, before coming to a round, concrete tank structure.

Turn left at the tank, and drive east. Turn right at the next intersection. Follow this major road for about 4.6 kilometers, into the forest. Turn left, and follow a terrible road east for 9.5 kilometers, crossing several rough creek bottoms on the way. At 9.5 kilometers, the road rises out of a river crossing and meets a grassy intersection. Turn right, and follow the rough road 2.3 kilometers. There is a radio tower on the left (north). From this point, a rough four-wheel-drive road leads southeast, over a ridge. Follow this road for several kilometers or as far as your vehicle can make it on the rough road.

TIMAU ROUTE: ROAD END TO MINTO'S HUT / DAY 1

Ascent: 3,300 meters to 4,300 meters
Distance: 16 kilometers
Time: 10 hours

The trail, where it exists, heads south, and slightly southeast, as it traverses around the tops of the Kazita East and Kazita West Valleys. The route follows the Kazita East Valley, the more southerly and larger of the two, in a southwesterly direction for about 3 kilometers, until it crests a high col and drops down into the Hinde Valley, where it crosses the north branch of the Nithi River, then continues south over relatively level country before joining the Chogoria Route at Minto's Hut. From this point, follow descriptions for the Chogoria Route.

SUMMIT CIRCUIT PATH

Although circumnavigations of Kibo on Kilimanjaro are not common, circumnavigations of the main peaks of Mount Kenya are extremely popular. This is mostly because Mount Kenya is much smaller than Kibo, and also because the forest and moorland routes to Mount Kenya's main peaks come in from all directions, so the Summit Circuit Path must be used to link together trails, huts, and routes. On Kili, most of the forest and moorland routes all come in from the south, so only the South Circuit Path is regularly used. On Mount Kenya, the Summit

Circuit Path is regularly used, and the entire cluster of main peaks on Mount Kenya can be easily circumnavigated in one day.

The following description of the Summit Circuit Path begins at the 4,300-meter intersection of the Naro Moru Route, near American Camp, since most people will first encounter the circuit path at this point, and will go around the mountain counterclockwise. This circumnavigation includes about 2,132 meters of elevation gain and loss and about 10 kilometers of travel.

From the end of the Naro Moru Route in the upper Teleki Valley, the Summit Circuit Path seems more like a continuation of the Naro Moru Route than its own separate trail. From the unmarked junction of the two routes, the circuit path heads off up a major gravel hill far to the right of the main peaks, switchbacking and scrambling for a vertical gain of about 600 meters. This hill is easily the worst hiking experience you will ever have on Mount Kenya.

After cresting a ridge, the trail wanders through stacks of jumbled blocks and emerges at Austrian Hut (4,800 meters).

From Austrian Hut, the path drops down to the south, into the very top portion of the wide, beautiful Hobley Valley. The route cuts across the head of the valley on a rocky, but fairly level trail that leads to Tooth Col. From Tooth Col, the trail drops down the hill and soon reaches Square Tarn. The Chogoria Route joins the Summit Circuit Path here. From Square Tarn, the Summit Circuit Path heads north, crosses another (minor) junction with the Chogoria Route at Simba Tarn, then climbs up steeply over Simba Col (4,650 meters). The views of Batian and Nelion from Simba Col are terrific. The trail then drops down a steep, gravelly hill to Shipton's Camp.

From Shipton's Camp, a faint trail leads up the hill to the southwest, heading straight toward the main peaks. After an hour, it reaches Kami Hut, an old tin shack. Past Kami Hut, the trail heads west-southwest and climbs up switchbacks in fine scree before topping out on Hausberg Col (4,590 meters). Point Peter (4,757 meters) will be the obvious triangular peak just to the south. From Hausberg Col, it's a very steep descent into the upper Hausberg Valley, where the aptly named Oblong and Hausberg Tarns are located. The trail then climbs out of the valley, passing the north side of Point Pigott on the way, to crest a ridge at Arthur's Seat. After topping the ridge, the trail winds along a beautiful series of rock ledges before passing Emerald Tarn (off to the right down the valley), Nanyuki Tarn, and Hut Tarn. Two Tarn Hut is located at Hut Tarn, on the west side of the lake.

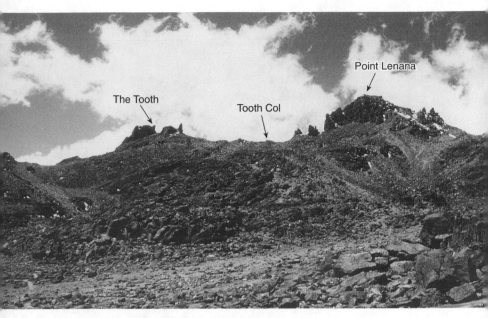

Tooth Col from Temple Fields, Chogoria Route, Mount Kenya
(Photo © Cameron M. Burns)

The Summit Circuit Path skirts the west side of Hut Tarn, then drops off into the Teleki Valley, down a steep hill to the south. At the bottom of this long hill is American Camp (4,350 meters). There are no facilities at American Camp, just a flat spot in the valley. Some parties bivouac here before attempting south-face routes on Nelion and Batian, like the Diamond Couloir (although it's better to hike up into the massive south-face amphitheater and bivouac closer to the routes).

From American Camp, the Summit Circuit Path continues south, where it meets the Naro Moru Route. There are about ten different variations of the trail between Two Tarn Hut, American Camp, and the upper part of the Naro Moru Route. A map and compass can be helpful in this area; however, just using the major landmarks is probably the easiest way to tell where you are.

As mentioned, the Summit Circuit Path can be done in one long day, or it can be broken up with overnight stops at any of the huts along the way. Some parties spend 3 days circumnavigating the mountain. There is no technical climbing on any portion of the Summit Circuit Path, and it can be done in walking shoes.

MOUNT KENYA PEAKS

Contrary to the understanding most safari-going tourists visiting Kenya have of the mountain, Mount Kenya is not just one single peak. It is, in fact, a dizzying cluster of peaks, towers, and summits, each of which has its own unique character.

Although most climbers visiting the Mount Kenya area head for Point Lenana (4,985 meters/16,355 feet)—the third-highest summit, which can be walked up—or Batian (5,199 meters/17,058 feet) and Nelion (5,188 meters/17,021 feet)—the twin highest points of Mount Kenya, which require technical climbing equipment and skills—there are many other interesting peaks and towers with exceptional routes on them.

The hiking, scrambling, rock climbing, and ice climbing routes are all generally excellent on Mount Kenya. However, that doesn't necessarily mean the rock is always solid. In many places it's rotten and loose, and rockfall on climbing routes is very common.

Routes on Mount Kenya's various summits are described in the following sections according to the various summits. Point Lenana, the trekkers' peak, is described first. Next, Nelion and Batian are described together because many of the routes on these peaks (for example, the South Face or the Ice Window) can be climbed to either summit. Indeed, the Normal Route on Mount Kenya takes in both summits.

Following the descriptions of these three major summits, the most popular climbs on Mount Kenya's subsidiary summits are described in a clockwise direction around the massif.

POINT LENANA

Point Lenana (4,985 meters/16,355 feet) is the standard trekkers' peak and provides outrageous views of Batian and Nelion from its summit. It is most commonly climbed from Austrian Hut (4,800 meters), from which the summit is just a 45-minute walk to the northeast. However, there are dozens of different possibilities for an ascent of Lenana.

Many parties start very early from Mackinder's Camp (4,200 meters) and climb the hill (via the Summit Circuit Path) to Austrian Hut before sunrise, continue on up to the top of Point Lenana to watch the sun rise, then return to Mackinder's Camp before descending back down the Naro Moru Route.

Looking towards Hausberg Col from Arthur's Seat on the Summit Circuit Path, Mount Kenya (Photo © Cameron M. Burns)

Hausberg Col

Point Peter

Batian

Nelion

Krapf Rognon

Thomson's Flake

Point Thomson

1. Point Lenana, Southwest Ridge (Scramble)

From Austrian Hut (4,800 meters), the route to the summit follows the ridge to the right of the Lewis Glacier. There are many variations. It is important to stay as close to the ridge as possible. If you stray too close to the edge of the Lewis Glacier, you'll soon find that the gravelly slopes between the ridge and the glacier lie on top of ice. Go too close to the glacier and you'll be slipping and sliding. Point Lenana has a summit block, and 2-meter walls bar easy access to the very top (4,985 meters). The easiest way up this block is on the northwestern corner (on the left side, at the far end if you're coming from Austrian Hut), where the block is stepped and can be negotiated easily.

2. Point Lenana, North Ridge (Scramble)

Compared with the Southwest Ridge, this route is rarely used. It can be climbed from Shipton's Camp or can be combined with the Southwest Ridge in either direction for a traverse of the peak.

From Shipton's Camp (4,200 meters), the trail to Point Lenana climbs up a narrow gorge with a small stream running through it, just southeast of the camp. After breaking through this gorge, the route climbs a very steep hill via many switchbacks, and eventually reaches Harris Tarn. From Harris Tarn, the trail continues up the hill behind (west of) Harris Tarn, and moves left (south) before following a gully to the top of a ridge, the North Ridge of Lenana. Turn left and scramble up the summit block (4,985 meters). This route receives a lot of sunshine in the morning and is a much warmer experience than the Southeast Ridge.

NELION / BATIAN

Batian (5,199 meters/17,058 feet) is the true summit, the highest point on Mount Kenya. It is separated from Nelion (5,188 meters/17,021 feet—the second-highest summit) by a gap of only 140 meters, the famed and beautiful Gate of the Mists.

A note on Batian/Nelion descents: The best descent from Batian and Nelion for all routes has traditionally been via the Normal Route of ascent on Nelion (see below). That means, if you are on Batian, you must traverse back to Nelion to make the descent.

Main features of Mount Kenya from the east
(Photo © Cameron M. Burns)

Several years ago, a team of Austrian climbers created a standardized rappel route from the summit of Nelion, which diverges slightly from the Normal Route. This rappel route, comprised of stainless steel rappel rings, is almost free of rockfall. From the summit of Nelion, follow the green paint markers to the first rappel. The other rappels should be obvious. One word of caution, however: on the second rappel (easily identified because it's the steepest), make sure your ropes are well placed over the edge of the ledge. They easily get caught!

According to national park officials, there are plans for another rappel route, down the Southern Slabs area on the south face of Batian.

3. Normal Route (Grade IV)

The Normal Route is standard for ascents of Nelion and Batian. It was first climbed by Eric Shipton and Percy Wyn Harris on January 6, 1929. Today, the route is generally climbed in twenty roped pitches and gains some 400 meters of elevation. Most parties climb Batian in 2 days and

Southeast Face of Nelion, Mount Kenya, with Route 3 marked
(Photo © Cameron M. Burns)

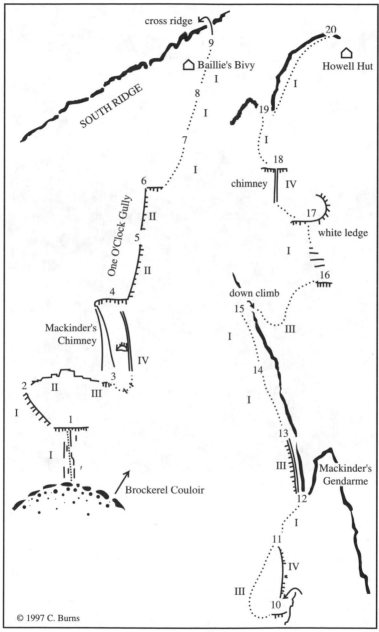

Normal Route to the summit of Nelion

© 1997 C. Burns

Benny Bach climbing Nelion from Gate of the Mists, Mount Kenya
(Photo © Cameron M. Burns)

Nelion in 1 day. It should be noted that when Halford Mackinder made the first ascent of Mount Kenya in 1899, he climbed portions of this route before traversing over the long South Ridge of Nelion and crossing the upper Darwin Glacier on the south side of Nelion, then angling up to the Diamond Glacier, the Gate of the Mists, and the summit of Batian.

The route begins in a small amphitheater (4,800 meters) above the Lewis Glacier, between the Brocherel Couloir and Point Melhuish. The amphitheater is more or less straight across the Lewis Glacier from Austrian Hut.

The first pitch (often climbed unroped) ascends a low-angled, well-worn wall (Grade I) in the back (north side) of the amphitheater to a huge ledge covered with broken boulders. The second pitch (also very easy) follows a left-angling gully that leads up from the left (west) end of the ledge. This gully is often filled with snow or ice, but it is easy to negotiate these sections in rock shoes. There is a dead Sykes monkey frozen under the ice in this gully, and its tail regularly appears sticking out from under the ice. Reportedly, it was coaxed with food all the way from the Naro Moru Gate up to the main peaks by British soldiers stationed in Nanyuki in August 1996. The soldiers then tried to lure the monkey up the Normal Route, but it died—apparently from exposure—on the second pitch.

At the top of this short pitch, an unlevel ledge is reached, the normal roping-up point. Pitch 3 traverses blocks—climbing up, down, and sideways—to the right, then steps across an airy drop to reach the base of Mackinder's Chimney. Mackinder's Chimney is very steep, and is often ice filled. It is rarely climbed and is not recommended.

From the base of the chimney, pitch 4 climbs down 3 meters and right about 10 meters, passing old pitons on the way, then straight up a low-angled crack that bypasses the right side of a triangular roof. Atop pitch 4 is a huge ledge and the One O'Clock Gully, which leads up and right for two pitches. After climbing two rope lengths up the gully (100 meters), move right onto a prominent flat block, which has many slings attached to it. Pitch 7 leads up and right onto easy (Grade I) ground. Climb two more very easy pitches up and right to Baillie's Bivy, the ruinous metal hut sitting on the crest of Nelion's South Ridge. Sleeping in the hut is not advised.

From Baillie's Bivy, pitch 10 crosses the crest of the South Ridge and descends about 25 meters onto rock ledges above the Upper Darwin Glacier. From this point, your goal is the notch between Mackinder's Gendarme and the upper South Ridge.

You can either climb rock straight up for two pitches, following the left side of the gendarme (there are several fixed pitons) at Grade IV, or skirt the rock by descending down to the steep, obvious snow gully to the left (Grade III), then scrambling up to the notch. Pitch 13 is a perfect crack in a shallow dihedral, directly above the notch. Climb loose blocks and ledges up the ridge above for two pitches (100 meters), until the wall above steepens. Down and to the right is an inobvious traverse (pitch 16) that is the key to routefinding. Climb down 20 meters, then traverse right to gain easy ground and several big ledges.

Follow one pitch up and left, in the obvious gully, to a broad, flat, white-colored ledge. The short Grade IV chimney to the left (north) is the last crux on the route and cannot be climbed with a pack on.

Above the chimney, scramble up and left on easy ground until you are overlooking the Diamond Glacier. A short, easy pitch up and right takes you to the summit of Nelion (5,188 meters/17,021 feet).

If you are planning to cross the Gate of the Mists and ascend Batian, a night in Howell Hut on Nelion's summit is highly recommended. The hut is very low, but well built, and offers foam padding (albeit dirty) on the floor. It can comfortably hold four people.

From Nelion's summit, scramble down the ridge 18 meters, then move to the right (east) side of the ridge. (Belaying is advisable.) The descent quickly turns from rock to ice, and crampons are highly recommended. Continue down into the Gate of the Mists by rappelling. If you have not brought crampons, you'll want to leave a rope fixed down the last section of ice leading to the col, as it is fairly steep (about 70 degrees). Cross the Gate of the Mists, then skirt the huge gendarme that sits on the Batian side of the Gate of the Mists to its right (north-east). Climb back up to the South Ridge. Generally, crampons and ice gear can be left here for the return trip to Nelion. Several easy short pitches climb the left side of Batian's South Ridge and lead to the summit (5,199 meters).

NELION / BATIAN SOUTH FACE

The following climbs on Batian/Nelion's South Face start in the huge, 600-meter-tall south-face amphitheater (4,600 meters) that contains the Diamond Couloir and Ice Window Routes.

It is best to bivouac at American Camp (4,350 meters) or higher, or to spend the night at Two Tarn Hut (4,500 meters) before starting these ascents. Most parties can do these routes in 1 day, but many people bivouac in the ice cave that is the Ice Window's namesake or on the summit of Batian or Nelion, to make the descent more leisurely.

South Face of Mount Kenya with Routes 4, 5, and 6 marked
(Photo © Cameron M. Burns)

4. SOUTH FACE ROUTE (GRADE IV)

The first ascent of the South Face Route was made by Arthur Firmin and John W. Howard in 1946. Originally Firmin and Howard climbed a line right of the lower section of the Ice Window Route, up the rock buttress between the Allan/Howell Variation (4A) and the Ice Window Route. Most modern parties climb the lower section of the Ice Window, then traverse right.

Like most other routes in this area, this route can be used to reach either Batian or Nelion, or both. It is usually climbed in about ten roped pitches, with much scrambling.

Start on the right side of the Lower Darwin Glacier, at about 4,600 meters, and climb it into a steep amphitheater that sits below the icefall joining the Upper and Lower Darwin Glaciers. Climb into the amphitheater's upper left-hand corner, where an obvious ramp leads up and left. Old slings and pieces of rope will make the route obvious. Turn the corner to join the lower section of the Ice Window icefall. A rocky gully just to the icefall's right can also be climbed. After several pitches, easy ground allows one to move right, to the bottom of the Upper Darwin Glacier. At the top of the Upper Darwin Glacier, move left, to the top of a rocky buttress overlooking the Diamond Glacier. This is where Mackinder's Original Route joins the South Face Route. The Diamond Glacier can be crossed diagonally, or it is possible to climb up to the Gate of the Mists, then continue on to Batian (5,199 meters) from there.

5. THE ICE WINDOW (GRADE V)

One of the true classics on the mountain, the Ice Window Route was first climbed by Phil Snyder, B. LeDain, and Y. Laulan on August 20, 1973.

Follow the description for the South Face until the lower part of the Ice Window icefall (4,800 meters) is gained. Follow the icefall for a half-dozen pitches to a large, icy cave protected by icicles. It is possible, though not recommended, to bivouac in the cave. Exit the cave at its left end by chopping a hole in the icicles and turn the lip of the cave to gain the lower end of the Diamond Glacier. Four to five pitches lead to the Gate of the Mists. Altogether, most parties climb fifteen to eighteen pitches roped.

6. DIAMOND COULOIR (GRADE VI)

Easily the most beautiful ice climb in Africa, the Diamond Couloir was first climbed by Phil Snyder and P. Thumbi on October 4–5, 1973. The first woman to climb the route was Hillary Collins, in 1976. The route has also been soloed several times. Yvon Chouinard and Michael Covington climbed the ice Headwall directly below the Diamond Glacier, which creates a direct route, in January 1975.

The route—a striking ribbon of steep ice—starts above the left (northwest) side of the Lower Darwin Glacier, at the 4,750-meter level. The first section of the route is steep and can be almost entirely rock during dry years. Atop the first pitch is a piton belay on the left side of the couloir. At the top of the second pitch is a cave that can be used for a bivouac. Four to five leads above the first cave, the route splits, with the original route leading out left on a ramp and the Headwall (6A) directly above. Both routes meet again on the Diamond Couloir. There is a second cave on the original route on the lower left side of the Diamond Glacier, which can be used as a bivouac.

Most parties climb fifteen to eighteen roped pitches.

7. SOUTHERN SLABS (GRADE VI-)

First climbed by Robert "Rusty" Baillie and R. M. Kamke on January 4, 1961, this route ascends the low-angled slabs left of the Diamond Couloir.

Starting from the 4,700-meter level in the huge south-face amphitheater, climb the Darwin Glacier's left (west) side, then the easy, right-trending ramp left of the bottom of the Diamond Couloir. When the ramp gets to within 12 meters of the Diamond Couloir, climb up a steep dihedral (Grade V) to the left for one pitch. Continue up a slab to a short wall, which is climbed on its left. Traverse right around a rib to another slab, and climb the slab to another short wall. Traverse left into a corner and up to a bulging face which is climbed by cracks (VI-) to a stance.

Traverse 30 meters right into a gully and climb the gully for 30 meters to a prominent ledge. Continue up and right following a gully and slabs for 60 meters. Climb the overhang above via the obvious chockstone on the left. Above is a yellow face. About 100 meters from the left-hand edge of this face is a hidden chimney, which is climbed to a traverse to the right, then an obvious crack. Climb down and right to a ledge, then traverse right to a slab. Climb the slab, then the 5-meter wall above to gain another ledge. Traverse down and right into a steep gully. Climb the gully to a sloping ledge, then traverse left onto a block, and climb the face above the block.

Above are two steep gullies leading to the Southwest Ridge. Climb the right-hand gully to join the ridge and follow it to the summit of Batian (5,199 meters).

Portions of this route can be ice covered, and crampons are recommended. There are currently plans to make this route the standard descent route from Batian.

Most parties take 1 to 2 days for this ascent.

8. DIAMOND BUTTRESS (GRADE VI, A1 OR GRADE VII)

This is the classic outing on the Diamond Buttress, the large wall left of the Diamond Couloir. The first ascent was by John Temple and Ian Howell on March 13–14, 1976.

From Two Tarn Hut (4,500 meters), climb up the left-hand edge of the Darwin Glacier. On the right side of the Diamond Buttress is a prominent corner. Climb it for three pitches to a wall. Move left and up into a chimney that splits. Follow the left branch of the chimney to its top, then move right and climb a short wall to a ledge. Move right to a crack and climb it (VI) until a pendulum allows one to traverse right across a blank wall and into a chimney. Done free, this traverse is Grade VII.

At the top of the chimney are several bivouac sites on ledges. Above the ledges, move left up slabs to an obvious corner. Climb the corner, then traverse left about 30 meters to the base of another crack. Climb the crack, and continue up and left for several pitches to a short chimney that gains a leftward-leaning ramp. Climb the ramp to a blank slab. Traverse right across a steep wall and around a corner into a crack system, then climb up to a ledge. Traverse right to a thin crack and climb it to a ledge. Climb the wall above the ledge, passing the overhang by going left (Grade VI). Several pitches of scrambling lead up and left to gain the Southwest Ridge, which is followed to the summit of Batian (5,199 meters).

Most parties take 1 long day or 2 short days to complete this route.

9. SOUTHWEST RIDGE (GRADE IV)

This route was first climbed by Arthur Firmin and John W. Howard, on January 8, 1946. It was probably first soloed by Dave Cheesmond in the mid-1970s.

From Two Tarn Hut (4,500 meters), climb up into the huge amphitheater below the Diamond Couloir and other south-face routes. Climb up the left (west) side of the Darwin Glacier until easy slabs allow one to scramble up to the notch between Point Slade (a subsidiary summit) and Batian. Climb the ridge above until it is possible to traverse left across an amphitheater to a minor ridge separating the amphitheater from the west face. Climb a steep buttress at the head of the amphitheater and follow the crest of the ridge to the summit of Batian (5,199 meters).

This route can easily be climbed in a day.

10. WEST FACE (GRADE V)

This classic route was first climbed by R. A. Caukwell and G. W. Rose on January 7, 1955. It was probably first soloed by Dave Cheesmond in the mid-1970s.

From Two Tarn Hut (4,500 meters), climb the Tyndall Glacier to an obvious snow slope that leads up and right between the Forel and Heim Glaciers. Climb the slope to a rib on the upper portion of the face, then climb past the rib to the right and continue up to the summit of Batian (5,199 meters). There are many options.

This route requires 1 full day to ascend.

11. THE UNTRAVELLED WORLD (GRADE VI)

This difficult and serious route was first climbed by Robert Barton and David Morris on January 10–11, 1978.

From Two Tarn Hut (4,500 meters), climb to the top of the Tyndall Glacier. From the top of the glacier, a thin gully leads to the lower left-hand edge of the hanging seracs of the Forel Glacier, above.

Climb the thin gully for four pitches, then make an exposed traverse right to gain a right-trending ramp that leads up and through the serac barrier to the Forel Glacier proper. Climb the Forel Glacier to its top, then climb several difficult mixed pitches up and right (west) to gain the Southwest Ridge. A scramble leads to the summit of Batian (5,199 meters).

Allow 2 days for the ascent.

12. WEST RIDGE (GRADE V)

The first ascent of the West Ridge, one of the most classic climbs on Mount Kenya, was made on August 1, 1930, by Eric Shipton and Bill Tilman.

The easiest and most straightforward approach is from Kami Hut (4,400 meters). Hike up to the base of the Northey Glacier and traverse up and right (west) along the west side of the glacier to the col between the Petit Gendarme and Point Dutton. From the col, climb up and left, on easy slabs, toward the summit of the Petit Gendarme. Follow moderate rock on the south side of the crest until just below the summit of the

Petit Gendarme, where an easy route leads around to the north and down into a spectacular exposed notch. A short wall leads up and left to an obvious bivy ledge. From the ledge, traverse up and along the base of the Grand Gendarme for several exposed but easy pitches. When the wall steepens, look for a ledge that leads right to a corner system that rises for 60 meters to the top of the Grand Gendarme.

Two difficult pitches (V) end at a comfortable but exposed ledge atop the gendarme. From here, follow the ridge crest for about 40 meters to the base of the "12 Meter Pinnacle." A few strenuous moves (V) on the left side of the pinnacle lead to easier rock and the arete. Follow this until it is possible to rappel into Shipton's Notch. A short, steep wall (with the only poor-quality rock on the entire route) leads out of the notch and back onto the ridge crest. Follow the right (south) side of the ridge for about four pitches to the summit of Batian (5,199 meters). Descend by the Normal Route on Nelion.

This route requires 1 to 2 days.

13. North Face Standard Route (Grade IV +)

This is the standard route used by climbers during the Northern Hemisphere's summer. The first ascent was made by Arthur Firmin and P. H. Hicks on July 31, 1944.

From Kami Hut (4,400 meters), traverse south along the east side of the mountain, and up into the wide gully between the Krapf Rognon and the main peak. A circle with a cross in it is chipped into the rock at the start of the route.

Climb up 10 meters, then move right (don't go left!) into a couloir. Follow the couloir for about 60 meters, and continue up to a right-facing corner that is climbed for 30 meters to easy slabs. On the slabs, move right about 5 meters to gain a series of easy grassy ledges below a wall. Continue up and left, then traverse right to a steep chimney that leads to a large hanging amphitheater that looks down on both the east and north sides of the mountain. This is where many parties bivouac on the route.

Traverse left across the amphitheater and climb an easy slabby gully that leads up and left. Near the top of the gully, traverse back right and up to the base of Firmin's Tower. Climb the left of two cracks on Firmin's Tower for 20 meters, then move to the right crack, a chimney, for 15

West Face of Mount Kenya with Routes 9–12 marked
(Photo © Cameron M. Burns)

East Face of Mount Kenya with Routes 13–15 and 26 marked
(Photo © Cameron M. Burns)

meters, then move left again into the first crack for 10 meters. Easy scrambling leads to the top of Firmin's Tower.

From the top of the tower, follow the ridge to a steep wall and climb up this to the right, where another, smaller, amphitheater is gained. Continue up the ridge above the amphitheater to reach the West Ridge proper, where there is an excellent bivouac site. Traverse left on easy ground to Shipton's Notch. From Shipton's Notch, traverse left on ledges to reach the summit of Batian (5,199 meters).

Allow 1 full day for the ascent. This route can also be used as a descent route.

14. FRENCH ROUTE (GRADE V, A1)

This route was first climbed by Maurice Martin and Roger Rangaux on August 28, 1952.

From Kami Hut (4,400 meters), traverse up and left below the start of the North Face Standard Route, to the next obvious gully. Climb 3 meters up a corner to a traverse leading right. At the end of the traverse, climb a chimney to reach a low-angled gully. Scramble up the gully for about 100 meters to another chimney, which is climbed by its right side.

Above the chimney, easy ledges lead to a dike, which is followed into the main gully. Climb up and right to a ledge. Continue up and right to a large corner, which is followed for 50 meters to the lower end of the huge Lower Amphitheater, which is filled with loose blocks. Climb up the left side of the amphitheater to its top, where an obvious ledge sits below a crack with old pitons, the Piton Crack.

Aid up the crack for 12 meters (A1) to a stance, then traverse left for a few meters to the base of an arete. Climb the arete (Grade V+), then a short crack that leads to a chimney. Climb the chimney to the Upper Amphitheater, then scramble up to the West Ridge. Scrambling leads to the summit of Batian (5,199 meters).

This route requires 1 to 2 days.

15. NORTHEAST PILLAR OF NELION (GRADE V, A1 OR GRADE VI+)

This, the first route on Mount Kenya's east face, was first climbed by Barry Cliff and Denis Rutowitz on August 2–4, 1963.

The climb starts at the base of Nelion's northeast prow, which lies just left of the huge Supercouloir that splits the mountain and divides Batian from Nelion. Set into the Krapf Glacier—which lies between the rounded Krapf Rognon and Nelion itself—is a large block, 15 meters away from the foot of the prow and near the start of the route, which follows a prominent crack, the Hourglass Crack.

Climb the face left of the crack and join it at a height of about 25 meters. Climb the crack until overhangs bar further upward progress, then move up and left to join the crest of a ridge. Climb 15 meters up the ridge to join a ramp, which is followed for 120 meters to the foot of the enormous Grey Pillar, a huge, square-shaped buttress. Traverse up and right around the Grey Pillar to two cracks, the right one very obvious, the left one not so obvious. The route follows the left one, which is also called Sinister Crack.

To start, climb up and left on blocks to a stance. Then, climb up and left, gaining the crack itself before reaching a stance. Follow the crack on the right wall above the stance to another stance, next to a loose flake. Continue up for another 40 meters to another stance. Climb up 30 meters, then traverse left to the shoulder of the Grey Pillar.

Continue up and right to a steep corner that can be climbed on aid or free at Grade VI, to reach good ledges. Above the corner, traverse left to a large, gray, featureless slab with a crack in it. Climb the crack to a fixed piton, then pendulum across the slab. Above the slab, a short crack leads to a stance below the final chimney. Climb the chimney and scramble up to the summit of Nelion (5,188 meters).

This ascent is usually done in 1 long day or 2 shorter days.

16. Eastern Groove of Nelion (Grade VI, A1)

This route was first climbed by Ian Howell and Iain Allan on June 2–3, 1978. A very fine route, with 600 meters of excellent rock, it has been free climbed.

The route starts 15 meters left of the Northeast Pillar of Nelion. Climb a very smooth, obvious slab, which leads to more slabs and a cave. Climb left, out of the cave, and climb up and right on slabs, then turn a corner to the right (Grade V). Continue up a few meters more to a recess. Climb the steep crack above the recess (one point of aid), then climb up a left-sloping ramp to a mantle. Scramble up to the base of an off-width crack, which is climbed (one point of aid) to easier ground and a large ledge. Traverse left along the ledge for 90 meters until you are 15 meters from the left-hand edge of the ledge. Above will be the Grey Corner; just left of the Grey Corner is the Eastern Groove, a wide, obvious crack with a rounded flake forming its left side.

Two pitches lead to the base of the Groove. Climb the Groove for four pitches of stemming, jamming, and laybacking. Some aid points are generally used. Climb a fifth pitch by laybacking (Grade V+) up to a phallus-shaped rock. Above this rock, climb slabs up to a steep corner with a crack. Avoid this crack by going left to an off-width crack around the corner. Climb the off-width (several aid points), then traverse back around to the right. Continue up for two pitches to a large ledge. Traverse right on the ledge for one pitch, to the base of a gully filled with loose blocks. Climb the gully to a chimney on the right. Climb the chimney and then scramble to the summit of Nelion (5,188 meters).

This route is generally climbed in 2 days.

17. EAST FACE ROUTE (GRADE VI, A3)

This route follows a series of cracks that runs from the summit of Nelion down the east face to the Krapf Glacier. It was first climbed by Heinrich Klier, Siegfried Aerberli, and Barry Cliff on August 7, 1963.

From the Krapf Glacier, climb two pitches in an obvious corner, to a big stance. The third pitch (called the Inverted Staircase) is a series of overhangs and the crux of the route. Above the overhangs is another stance, above which the right wall is climbed for 15 meters, followed by a traverse to the left for 3 meters.

Climb up a series of blocks to the Raven's Nest, a bivouac site. From the Raven's Nest, climb up and right to a stance. Continue up and right to an overhang (VI), then a difficult crack to a traverse left, around a corner to a stance. Climb above the stance for 5 meters, then move left into an overhang. Climb the overhang and the slab above to the bottom of a prominent gully.

Climb the gully for three pitches, then move to the gully's left side, which offers easier climbing. Above will be the Black Crack, a prominent chimney that leads to the summit. To reach the Black Crack, climb two pitches of cracks that lead up and right. The Black Crack starts as a chimney (VI-) for 15 meters, then becomes overhanging for 10 meters (A3), before a ledge is gained on the left. One more pitch with a few aid moves leads to easy scrambling and the summit of Nelion (5,188 meters).

Allow 1 long day or 2 short days for an ascent.

POINT MELHUISH

Point Melhuish is a rounded hump sitting on Nelion's South Ridge, between the Normal Route on Nelion/Batian and Point John.

Point John, Point John Minor, Point Melhuish, and Nelion, showing Routes 3, 18–20, and 22 (Photo © Cameron M. Burns)

18. Point Melhuish, East Side (Scramble)

Point Melhuish (4,880 meters/16,010 feet) can be ascended by an easy scramble up its eastern edge. From Austrian Hut (4,800 meters), cross the Lewis Glacier to the southeast side of Point Melhuish and scramble up ledges on the right side of the formation.

Point John

After Point Lenana and Nelion, Point John (4,883 meters/16,020 feet) probably sees more traffic than any other summit on the Mount Kenya massif. Although small, it is a fantastic spire, comparable to any of the world's most spectacular rock peaks.

19. Point John, Southeast Gully (Grade III)

This popular route—the standard route up Point John—was first climbed by Eric Shipton and Pat Russell on December 18, 1929.

The route follows the wide, scoured gully on the southeast face, directly below the summit. There are five pitches, with multiple cruxes, but none are harder than about Grade III. Descent is made by rappelling the route. There are many rappel anchors.

20. Point John, South Ridge (Grade III)

From American Camp or Austrian Hut (4,800 meters), walk to the base of the southeast gully and traverse left. Climb up and left to an obvious white spot on the South Ridge. Follow steep rock up and right for several pitches to the top of the first tower. Continue climbing diagonally up past more towers to reach the summit. This route is generally climbed in six to seven pitches.

21. Point John, Point John Couloir (Grade V)

The first ascent of this route was by Phil Snyder and D. Karinga, in May 1972.

When it's in condition, this is one of the finest ice routes on the mountain. It is in the huge south-face amphitheater that contains the Diamond Couloir and Ice Window Routes and is just downhill and right of those two routes. More specifically, it lies on the north side of the South Ridge of Nelion, at the point where the South Ridge joins Point John Minor. The ice is continuous for the entire 180 meters of the route. There are very few fixed anchors, and the route is in the best condition from December through March.

The best descent is to climb through the notch on the South Ridge, then scramble and rappel down the south side of the ridge. (This descent is also the Original Route on Point John Minor.)

22. POINT JOHN MINOR, ORIGINAL ROUTE (GRADE V)

Point John Minor (4,875 meters/15,994 feet) is a subsidiary summit of Point John, lying on Point John's northeast side. The Original Route climbs the obvious long gully on the South Ridge of Nelion, leading to a notch between Point John Minor and the jumbled rock outcrops south of Point Melhuish (right of the notch).

It's three and a half pitches of easy scrambling to the notch. At the notch, turn left, and climb straight up for 16 meters (V). About 30 meters above the notch, on the left, is a steep, wide crack with chockstones. Climb it to the top. Bring rappel anchors. After two rappels, the Southeast Gully on Point John is met, and it's possible to rappel that route to the bottom of Point John.

The Original Route is best climbed from Austrian Hut (4,800 meters), from December through March, although there can be snow on the upper part of the route.

MIDGET PEAK

Midget Peak (4,700 meters/15,420 feet) lies just west of Point John, and is a small, oblong-shaped tower standing on its end.

23. MIDGET PEAK, SOUTH GULLY (GRADE IV)

The first ascent of this, the standard route, was made in August 1930 by Eric Shipton and Bill Tilman.

On the south face of Midget Peak is a big gully, the South Gully. The first 25 meters follow an obvious crack. Above the crack, scramble up 18 meters to an area of columnar rock. Several short pitches lead to an obvious cave. Climb up the left side of the cave to a prominent ledge, then climb the right wall above the ledge, then traverse left on a sloping ledge to another wide ledge. Continue left, then climb a bulge via a 6-meter crack, followed by a sloping slab that puts one over the north face. Climb up and around several large blocks to reach the summit. The best descent is to climb down a few meters toward the col between Point John and Midget Peak, then rappel.

Cam Burns on the Point John Couloir, Mount Kenya
(Photo © Benny Bach)

Point Peter, Mount Kenya, showing Route 24
(Photo © Cameron M. Burns)

POINT PETER

Point Peter (4,757 meters/15,607 feet) is the spectacular triangular spire just south of Hausberg Col and southwest of Kami Hut.

24. POINT PETER, SOUTH RIDGE (GRADE V)

The first ascent of this route was made by Eric Shipton and Bill Tilman in July 1930.

From Kami Hut (4,400 meters), climb up to the col between Point Peter and Point Pigott. Turn right to face Point Peter. The first pitch follows the arete for about 18 meters, then traverses right on big, loose-looking holds to a belay. A strenuous move off the ledge (Grade V) leads to nice, steep face climbing, followed by an easy ridge leading to the summit.

The best descent is via the Northeast Ridge. Scramble down 16 meters to the northeast, to rappel slings. Two rappels (25 meters and 22 meters), followed by some third-class scrambling, put you on the talus below the peak.

Allow 2 to 3 hours for this route.

POINT DUTTON

Point Dutton (4,885 meters/16,207 feet) is the large peak immediately south of Point Peter and on the northwest side of the Northey Glacier.

25. POINT DUTTON, NORTHEAST FACE–EAST RIDGE (GRADE V)

This route was first climbed by S. Barusso and R. Metcalfe in August 1966.

From Kami Hut (4,400 meters), approach the center of the northeast face. Scramble up the center of the northeast face for 60 meters, until a rope-up spot is reached. Two pitches of steep climbing with large holds lead above the Northey Glacier to an easy gully that goes back right to the base of an impressive finger. This marks the crux of the route. A few Grade V moves lead to easier climbing up steep cracks that end on the north summit. Three pitches along a spectacular exposed arete lead south to the actual high point. The best descent is down the steep North Ridge (Class 3).

The climb takes 6 hours.

KRAPF ROGNON

The Krapf Rognon (4,800 meters/15,748 feet) is a rounded hump of rock—similar to Point Melhuish—sitting below the northeast face of Nelion.

26. KRAPF ROGNON, SOUTHEAST SIDE (SCRAMBLE)

The Krapf Rognon can be ascended by an easy scramble up the south-eastern edge. Crampons are highly recommended. The summit offers excellent views of the east-face routes on Mount Kenya.

POINT THOMSON

Point Thomson (4,995 meters/16,388 feet) is Point Lenana's sister peak, and lies just west of the latter by a few hundred meters.

27. POINT THOMSON, EAST RIDGE (SCRAMBLE)

This climb is similar to Point Lenana's Southwest Ridge except that it involves serious glacier travel. Parties need crampons and ice axes, and should be roped because of crevasses on the upper Lewis Glacier.

The route is straightforward. Walk up the Lewis Glacier to the ridge between Point Lenana and Point Thomson, and scramble up the East Ridge to the summit. Allow a half day from Austrian Hut (4,800 meters).

THOMSON'S FLAKE

Thomson's Flake is the improbable spire between Point Thomson and Nelion's southeast face. It is rarely climbed.

28. THOMSON'S FLAKE, NORTH FACE (GRADE VI)

This route was first climbed by Leo Herncarek, Walter Welsch, and Barry Cliff in September 1962.

Start on the col (4,830 meters) between Point Thomson and Thomson's Flake, and climb up to the base of a chimney. Climb the corner on the left side to a ramp, traverse left along it to another corner. Climb this corner to reach a belay ledge. Climb the wall above the ledge to another ramp, then traverse right around a corner. Ascend the overhang above, then move up and right to the summit ridge. Scramble to the top. The best descent is to rappel the south face.

Allow half a day for this climb.

APPENDIX A
USEFUL ADDRESSES
& TELEPHONE NUMBERS

EMBASSIES
KENYAN EMBASSIES ABROAD

AUSTRALIA
Embassy of the Republic of Kenya
QBE Building
33 Ainslie Avenue
Canberra
ACT 2601
Telephone: 062-474788

CANADA
Embassy of the Republic of Kenya
415 Laurier Avenue
Ottawa
Ontario KIN 6R4
Telephone: 613-563-1773

TANZANIA
Embassy of the Republic of Kenya
NIC Investment House
Samora Avenue
P.O. Box 5231
Dar es Salaam
Phone: 46362 or 46366

UNITED KINGDOM
Embassy of the Republic of Kenya
45 Portland Place
London W1N 4AS
England
Telephone: 71-636-2371

UNITED STATES
Embassy of the Republic of Kenya
2249 R Street NW
Washington, DC 20008
Telephone: 202-387-6106 (Visa Section, ext. 3942 or 3945)

Tanzanian Embassies Abroad
UNITED STATES
Embassy of the United Republic of Tanzania
2139 R Street NW
Washington, DC 20008
Telephone: 202-939-6125

Foreign Embassies in Kenya
AUSTRALIA
Australian Commission
Riverside Drive, off Chiromo Road
P.O. Box 39341
Nairobi
Telephone: 445034
CANADA
Canadian High Commission
Comcraft House
Haile Selassie Avenue
P.O. Box 30481
Nairobi
Telephone: 214804
TANZANIA
Embassy of the United Republic of Tanzania
Continental House, at Uhuru Highway and Harambee Avenue
P.O. Box 47790
Nairobi
Telephone: 331056
UNITED KINGDOM
British High Commission
Upper Hill Road
P.O. Box 30465
Nairobi
Telephone: 714699
UNITED STATES
United States Embassy
Moi Avenue at Haile Selassie Avenue
P.O. Box 30137
Nairobi
Telephone: 334141

Foreign Embassies in Tanzania

AUSTRALIA
   (Contact the Canadian High Commission in Dar es Salaam.
   See below)

CANADA
   Canadian High Commission
   38 Mirambo Street
   P.O. Box 1022
   Dar es Salaam
   Telephone: 112831

UNITED KINGDOM
   British High Commission
   Hifadhi House
   Samora Avenue
   P.O. Box 30465
   Dar es Salaam
   Telephone: 51296015

NATIONAL PARKS

Kenya
   Mount Kenya National Park
   P.O. Box 69
   Naro Moru
   Kenya
   (No telephone listed)

Tanzania
   Kilimanjaro National Park
   P.O. Box 96
   Marangu
   Tanzania
   Telephone: 50 in Tanzania

SHUTTLE OPERATORS

Kenya
   Davanu Car Hire and Tours
   4th Floor, Windsor House

University Way
P.O. Box 9081
Nairobi
Telephone: 222002 or 217178
Fax: 557274 or 216475
(Operators of the Davanu shuttle between Nairobi and Moshi)

TANZANIA

Davanu Car Hire and Tours
Adventure Centre
Gollondoi Road
Arusha
Telephone: 255-57-8142
Fax: 255-57-4311

OUTFITTERS

KILIMANJARO

The following outfitters—in this order—were recommended by
Kilimanjaro National Park warden Matthew Mombo. I concur with his
list, and have either used them myself or heard excellent reports about
all the companies listed.

ZARA Tanzania Adventures
P.O. Box 1990
Moshi
Tanzania
Telephone: 255-55-54240 or 50808
Fax: 255-55-53105, 50233, or 50011
Email: zara@form-net.com

ZARA has an office inside the Moshi Hotel, opposite where the Davanu
shuttle drops off in Moshi, as well as their main office just around the
corner to the west. Regarded by both Kilimanjaro National Park officials and this author as "the best" company offering guided climbs of
Kilimanjaro. (Zainab and Roger Ansell, owners/operators)

MJ Safaris International
P.O. Box 558
Moshi
Tanzania

Telephone: 255-55-52017 or 51241
Fax: 255-55-50096
(Thomas Lyimo, managing director)
MJ Safaris has an office located in the YMCA building. The company was operating under the name Trans Kibo for many years, and is well known. Thomas Lyimo, the manager, has decades of experience in tourism and mountain climbing.

Shah Tours and Travel, Ltd.
P.O. Box 1821
Moshi
Tanzania
Telephone: 255-55-2370
Shah Tours and Travel has an office located on Mawenzi Road, in Moshi.

Marangu Hotel
P.O. Box 40
Moshi
Tanzania
Telephone: 11 in Marangu

MOUNT KENYA

Michael Wanjau, who works in Park Warden Bongo Woodley's office, compiled the following list.

Kenya's Mountain Scene Club
P.O. Box 461
Chogoria
Kenya

Mount Kenya Chogoria Porters and Guides Association
P.O. Box 114
Chogoria
Kenya

Mount Kenya Muthambi Guides and Porters Club
P.O. Box 73
Chogoria
Kenya

Mount Kenya Guides and Porters Safari Club
P.O. Box 128
Naro Moru
Kenya

Tourist Safari Guides and Porters Club
P.O. Box 56
Naro Moru
Kenya

Naro Moru Safari Camp Guides
P.O. Box 145
Naro Moru
Kenya

Old Moses Porters and Guides Club
P.O. Box 333
Nanyuki
Kenya

MAP AND GUIDEBOOK SOURCES

UNITED KINGDOM
West Col Productions
Goring
Reading RG8 9AA
England

Cordee
3a DeMontfort Street
Leicester LE1 7HD
England

UNITED STATES
Chessler Books
P.O. Box 4359
Evergreen, CO 80437
U.S.A.
Telephone: 1-800-654-8502; or 303-670-0093

Adventurous Traveler Bookstore
P.O. Box 64769
Burlington, VT 05406-4769
1-800-282-3963; or 802-860-6776
Email: books@atbook.com

NAIROBI HOTELS

Boulevard Hotel
Harry Thuku Road
Telephone: 337221
Fax: 334071
About US$80 per night.

The New Stanley Hotel
Corner of Kimathi Street and Kenyatta Avenue
Telephone: 333248
Fax: 211472
Right in the heart of the city. The hotel's famous Thorn Tree Cafe is one of Ernest Hemingway's old haunts and a great place to people watch. US$120 per night.

Norfolk Hotel
Harry Thuku Road
Telephone: 335422
Fax: 22559
About US$225 per night.

Oakwood Hotel
Kimathi Street and Kenyatta Avenue
Telephone: 220592
Across Kimathi Street from the New Stanley. About US$60 per night. Nairobi's largest concentration of taxi drivers seems to congregate just outside the Oakwood, so it's a good place to arrange a taxi to Mount Kenya.

Suncourt Inn
University Way
Telephone: 221418
Fax: 217500
About US$50 per night for a double.

Nairobi YMCA
State House Road
Telephone: 724066
About US$10 per night.

Nairobi YWCA
  Mamlaka Road
  Telephone: 724699
  About US$10 per night.

MOUNT KENYA HUT RESERVATIONS

To reserve hut space on the Naro Moru Route (Meteorological Station
and Mackinder's Camp) contact:
Naro Moru River Lodge
  P.O. Box 18
  Naro Moru
  Kenya
  Telephone: 176-62622

Their Nairobi agents are:
Let's Go Travel
  Caxton House
  Standard Street
  P.O. Box 60342
  Nairobi
  Kenya
  Telephone: 330341

To reserve hut space on the Sirimon Route (Old Moses and Shipton's
Camp), contact:
Mountain Rock Lodge
  P.O. Box 333
  Nanyuki
  Kenya
  Telephone: 176-62051, 62625, or 22134

Or, contact the Lodge's Central Reservations Office, in Nairobi:
Mountain Rock Lodge
  Central Reservation Office
  Jubilee Insurance House, 2nd Floor
  Wabera/Kaunda Street
  P.O. Box 40270
  Nairobi
  Kenya
  Telephone: 254-2-210051, 242133, or 242731
  Fax: 254-2-210051 or 242731

Kami Hut, with Terere and Sendeyo behind, Mount Kenya
(Photo © Cameron M. Burns)

APPENDIX B
GLOSSARY OF LOCAL LANGUAGES

ENGLISH	SWAHILI	MERU	KIKUYU
abseil (rappel)	kutemlemka kwamawe kutokajuu	kuikuruka	guikuruka
alpinist	mpandaji	mutuii	mutuii
to arrive (at the summit)	fika	gukinya	gukinya
aspirin	aspirini	aspirini	aspirini
baggage	mizigo	murigo	murigo
beer	bia	nchobi	njohi
to belay	kuteremsha	guturemukia	kuharurukia
bivouac	—	kurungaria	ngurunga
blizzard	—	kirorua	kiroruha
boots	buti	mbuti	mbuti
carabiners	karabina	gwati	gwati
campsite	kambi	kambi	kambi
cliff	mlima mdogo	karima	karima kanini
to climb	kupanda	gwitia	gutamba
the climb	upandaji	kwambata	uhaichi
the climber	mpandaji	mwitia	muhaichi
cloud	mawingu	matu	matu
col	m'gongo	ntumbii	—
cold	baridi	mpio	heho
compass	dira	kabachi	kabathi
crack	mwanya	mwatuka	mwatuka
crampons	viatu ya barafu	iratu bia barubu	iratu cia barabu
Danger!	Hatari!	Ugwati!	Uguati!
the descent	kuturemka	guteremuka	kuharuruka
doctor	daktari	gitari	rigitari
east	mashariki	kiumiriro	riumiriro
flashlight	tochi	tochi	tochi
flat	tambarare	muganano	mwaragano
fog	ukungu	mpundu	kibii
food	chakula	irio	irio

ENGLISH	SWAHILI	MERU	KIKUYU
frozen	kuganda	kuthita	kuganda
fuel	mafuta	maguta	maguta
gaiters	—	ngeta	ngeta
glacier	barafu nyingi	barabu	barabu
gloves	grobe	ngrobe	—
goggles	miwani ya barafu	machichio	machichio
guide	mwongozi	mutongoria	mutongoria
hammer	nyundo	nyondo	nyondo
headlamp	tochi ya kichwa	tochi ya kongo	tochi ya kongo
helmet	—	nkobia	ngobia
Help!	Msaada!	Gutethia!	Uteithio!
high	juu	iguru	iguru
hill	mlima kidogo	karima	karima
hut	nyumba kindogo	kanyumba	thingira
ice	barafu	mbarabu	barafu
ice ax	shoka ya barafu	ithanua ria mbrarbu	ithanua ria mbrarbu
injury	jeraha	gukururua	gutihio
jacket	kabuti	kabuti	kabuti
knife	kisu	gaciu	gahiu
knot	—	gikundo	gikundo
map	ramani	mabu	mabu
medicine	dawa	ndawa	ndawa
mountain	mlima	kirima	kirima
mountaineer	mpadaji	mwitia wairima	muhaichi kirima
no	hapana	gutiri	gutiri
north	kaskazini	ruguru	ruguru
pack	kusanya	kubanga	kubanga
pass	pita	gukuruka	kuhituka
petrol	petroli	beteruri	beturo
photo	picha	mbicha	mbicha
porter	wachukuzi	makamati wamirigo	mukui mirigo
rent	kodi	igoti	igoti
ridge	milima	gagaa kanini	tumu
road	barabara	barabara	barabara

ENGLISH	SWAHILI	MERU	KIKUYU
rock	jiwe	iga	ihiga
rockfall	mtelemro wa mawe	kwaruka kwa maiga	kiharuruko
rope	kamba	mukna	muknada
route	njia	njira	njira
scree	mawe kidogo	mwambatiro	tumahiga tunini
shovel	kipauro	giciko giatiri	giciko giatiri
ski	kiziwashiria kutekemka	kwirekiria mwimanoni	—
ski poles	viziti via kutelemka	tumititwa kwimana	—
sleeping bag	mfarishi	mubuka yakumama	muhuko wagukomera mukondoro
sleeping pad	ngondold	ithitho	—
snow	tharuji	nkamia	barafu
south	kusini	ihiriro	itherero
stake, peg	vishikio vya hema	ikingi ziaigema	—
steep	mutelemko milali	mwinamo	haruruko
Stop!	Simama!	Rugama!	Rugama!
stove	stofu	thitobu	thitobu
straps	nyuji	ndigii	—
stream	mto kidogo	kamwera	karui
summit	kilele	iguru	gathumbiri
sunburn	kuchomwa na jua	kuja ni riva	kuhia ni riua
sunburn cream	dawa ya ngozi	ndawa ya ngothi	ndawa ua ngothi
sunglasses	miwani ya jua	maitho ya riua	macicio ma riua
supermarket	supamaket	kathoko	thoko
tent	hema	kaema	hama
tent fly	kituniko cha hema	kiandavua	—
thirsty	kuwa na kiu	nyonta	kunyota
toilet	choo	—	—
trail	njia ya wanjama	tujira twa mbiti	njira ya nyamu
valley	bonde	kiolo	mukuri
village	kijij	ituura	gichagi
visa	viza	vija	—
Wait!	Ngoja!	Eterera!	Eterera!
wall	ukuta	ruthingo	ruthungo

ENGLISH	SWAHILI	MERU	KIKUYU
water	maji	ruji	mai
water bottle	chupa ya maji	cuba ya ruuji	cuba ya mai
weather	hali ya hewa	riera	riera
west	magharibi	muthiriro	ithuito
wind	upepo	rugo	ruhuho
yes	ndiyo	niu	iini
zipper	zipu	nyororo	nyororo

APPENDIX C
FURTHER READING

The following books are all recommended to further your understanding of East Africa and Kilimanjaro and Mount Kenya.

Allan, Iain, ed. *Guide to Mount Kenya and Kilimanjaro.* Nairobi: Mountain Club of Kenya, 1990. (P.O. Box 45741, Nairobi, Kenya.) Historically, the best reference for technical mountaineers available.

Benuzzi, Felice. *No Picnic on Mount Kenya.* Layton, Utah: Gibbs Smith, 1989. Originally published in 1953. A classic account of an unusual ascent of Point Lenana by three Italian prisoners of war in 1943. Benuzzi and his friends escaped from a British POW camp near Nanyuki to climb Mount Kenya, then escaped back into the camp after their ascent. Their route approximates the Burguret Route on the mountain.

Else, David. *Trekking in East Africa.* Hawthorn, Victoria: Lonely Planet, 1993. (P.O. Box 617, Hawthorn, Victoria, Australia.) A well-written, comprehensive guide to trekking on Kilimanjaro, Mount Kenya, and the Ruwenzoris. Technical climbing is not included.

Finlay, Hugh, and Geoff Crowther. *East Africa.* 4th ed. Hawthorn, Victoria: Lonely Planet, 1997. (P.O. Box 617, Hawthorn, Victoria, Australia.) A general guide to East Africa in which Lonely Planet's entire *Kenya* book is reprinted. Includes information on the most popular treks on Mount Kenya but does not include trekking on Kilimanjaro. Has good information on the towns of Moshi and Arusha, as well as traveling around Tanzania.

___. *Kenya.* Hawthorn, Victoria: Lonely Planet, 1994. (P.O. Box 617, Hawthorn, Victoria, Australia.) A general guide to Kenya, with excellent descriptions of Nairobi and the small towns around Mount Kenya. Also includes information on the most popular treks on Mount Kenya.

Mackinder, Halford. *The First Ascent of Mount Kenya.* Athens: Ohio University Press, 1991 (reprint). A diary-style record of Mackinder's first ascent of the peak in 1899.

Shipton, Eric. *Upon That Mountain.* England: Cordee, 1985 (reprint). An excellent account of Shipton's climbing activities in East Africa.

Swahili Phrase Book & Dictionary. Oxford, England: Berlitz, 1995.
(Peterley Road, Oxford, 0X4 2TX, England.) A good basic
overview of the most important Swahili words and expressions.

Taylor, Rob. *The Breach.* New York: Coward, McCann & Geoghan,
1981. An excellent account of an early attempt on Kilimanjaro's
Breach Wall.

Wielochowski, Andrew. *Kilimanjaro Map and Guide.* Halufryn,
Cilycwm, Wales: Executive Wilderness Programs, 1990. Similar to
Wielochowski and Savage's earlier *Mt Kenya Map and Guide.*
Includes a full-size topographic map and a condensed technical
mountaineering guide.

Wielochowski, Andrew, and Mark Savage. *Mt Kenya Map and Guide.*
Halufryn, Cilycwm, Wales: Executive Wilderness Programs, 1990.
This condensed technical mountaineering guide is generally
regarded as having the best maps of Mount Kenya, including a
full-sized topographic map.

INDEX

ABOUT THE AUTHOR

Colorado-based mountaineer and journalist, Cameron "Cam" Burns was born in Australia and spent the summers of his childhood roaming the mountains of Tasmania. In 1978 his family emigrated to the United States, where he learned technical climbing and earned a degree in architecture at the University of Colorado.

After working in the film industry in Hollywood for several years, he began writing fulltime. His articles, photographs, and fictional stories have been published in newspapers and magazines here and abroad. He is the author of *Colorado Ice Climber's Guide; The Maroon Bells: A Climbing Guide* (forthcoming); and co-author, with Steven Porcella, of *Climbing California's Fourteeners: The Route Guide to the Fifteen Highest Peaks*. He is married to Ann Robertson and lives in Basalt, Colorado.

THE MOUNTAINEERS, founded in 1906, is a nonprofit outdoor activity and conservation club, whose mission is "to explore, study, preserve, and enjoy the natural beauty of the outdoors. . . . " Based in Seattle, Washington, the club is now the third-largest such organization in the United States, with 15,000 members and five branches throughout Washington State.

The Mountaineers sponsors both classes and year-round outdoor activities in the Pacific Northwest, which include hiking, mountain climbing, ski-touring, snowshoeing, bicycling, camping, kayaking and canoeing, nature study, sailing, and adventure travel. The club's conservation division supports environmental causes through educational activities, sponsoring legislation, and presenting informational programs. All club activities are led by skilled, experienced volunteers, who are dedicated to promoting safe and responsible enjoyment and preservation of the outdoors.

If you would like to participate in these organized outdoor activities or the club's programs, consider a membership in The Mountaineers. For information and an application, write or call The Mountaineers, Club Headquarters, 300 Third Avenue West, Seattle, Washington 98119; (206) 284-6310.

The Mountaineers Books, an active, nonprofit publishing program of the club, produces guidebooks, instructional texts, historical works, natural history guides, and works on environmental conservation. All books produced by The Mountaineers are aimed at fulfilling the club's mission.

Send or call for our catalog of more than 300 outdoor titles:

The Mountaineers Books
1001 SW Klickitat Way, Suite 201
Seattle, WA 98134
1-800-553-4453
e-mail: mbooks@mountaineers.org
website: www.mountaineers.org

Other titles you may enjoy from The Mountaineers:

DENALI'S WEST BUTTRESS: A Climber's Guide, *Colby Coombs*
This definitive guide to the classic West Buttress Route features comprehensive, step-by-step expert instruction, plus Bradford Washburn's historic aerial photos.

K2: CHALLENGING THE SKY, *Kurt Diemburger*
A detailed photographic portfolio of the great mountain and its routes, covering the history of climbing K2 — the most dangerous and technically difficult mountain in the world to climb — from the earliest explorations up to the latest ascents.

HIMALAYA ALPINE-STYLE: The Most Challenging Routes on the Highest Peaks, *Andy Fanshawe & Stephen Venables*
Thorough in-depth text and remarkable color photographs enhance this large-format collector's edition, which explores the possibilities of the alpine-style approach in climbing the legendary peaks of the Himalaya and Karakoram.

A CLIMBER'S GUIDE TO THE TETON RANGE, 3d Ed.,
Leigh N. Ortenburger & Reynold G. Jackson
The preferred climbing guide to the Tetons for climbers of all levels of experience, including complete route descriptions for 800 routes on more than 200 peaks.

ACONCAGUA: A Climbing Guide, *R.J. Secor*
The only English-language guide to climbing the Western hemisphere's highest peak, including popular and less-tracked routes, advice on lodging, equipment, permits, and more, plus a Spanish mountaineering glossary.

THE MONT BLANC MASSIF: The 100 Finest Routes,
Gaston Rebuffat
Spectacular photographs highlight this classic, presenting Rebuffat's personal picks for 100 of the finest routes on the highest peak in western Europe.

Outdoor Books by the Experts

Whatever the season, whatever your sport, The Mountaineers Books has the resources for you. Our FREE CATALOG includes over 350 titles on climbing, hiking, mountain biking, paddling, backcountry skiing, snowshoeing, adventure travel, natural history, mountaineering history, and conservation, plus dozens of how-to books to sharpen your outdoor skills.

All of our titles can be found at or ordered through your local bookstore or outdoor store. Just mail in this card or call us at 800·553·4453 for your free catalog. Or send us an e-mail at mbooks@mountaineers.org.

Name _____

Address _____

City _____ State _____ Zip+4 _____ - _____

E-mail _____

557-3

Outdoor Books by the Experts

Whatever the season, whatever your sport, The Mountaineers Books has the resources for you. Our FREE CATALOG includes over 350 titles on climbing, hiking, mountain biking, paddling, backcountry skiing, snowshoeing, adventure travel, natural history, mountaineering history, and conservation, plus dozens of how-to books to sharpen your outdoor skills.

All of our titles can be found at or ordered through your local bookstore or outdoor store. Just mail in this card or call us at 800·553·4453 for your free catalog. Or send us an e-mail at mbooks@mountaineers.org.

Please send a catalog to my friend at:

Name _____

Address _____

City _____ State _____ Zip+4 _____ - _____

E-mail _____

557-3

BUSINESS REPLY MAIL
FIRST-CLASS MAIL   PERMIT NO. 85063   SEATTLE, WA

POSTAGE WILL BE PAID BY ADDRESSEE

THE MOUNTAINEERS BOOKS
1001 SW KLICKITAT WAY STE 201
SEATTLE WA 98134-9975

BUSINESS REPLY MAIL
FIRST-CLASS MAIL   PERMIT NO. 85063   SEATTLE, WA

POSTAGE WILL BE PAID BY ADDRESSEE

THE MOUNTAINEERS BOOKS
1001 SW KLICKITAT WAY STE 201
SEATTLE WA 98134-9975